The Urban Girl's Manifesto

Melody Biringer

The Urban Girl's Manifesto

We CRAVE Community.
At CRAVE Toronto we believe in acknowledging, celebrating, and passionately supporting local businesses. We know that, when encouraged to thrive, neighbourhood establishments enhance communities and provide rich experiences not usually encountered in mass-market. We hope that, by introducing you to the savvy business women in this guide, CRAVE Toronto will help inspire your own inner entrepreneur.

We CRAVE Adventure.
We could all use a getaway, and at CRAVE Toronto we believe that you don't need to be a jet setter to have a little adventure. There's so much to do and to explore right in your own backyard. We encourage you to break your routine, to venture away from your regular haunts, to visit new businesses, to explore all the funky finds and surprising spots that Toronto has to offer. Whether it's to hunt for a birthday gift, indulge in a spa treatment, order a bouquet of flowers, or connect with like-minded people, let CRAVE Toronto be your guide for a one-of-a-kind hometown adventure.

We CRAVE Quality.
CRAVE Toronto is all about quality products and thoughtful service. We know that a satisfying shopping trip requires more than a simple exchange of money for goods, and that a rejuvenating spa date entails more than a quick clip of the cuticles and a swipe of polish. We know you want to come away feeling uplifted, beautiful, excited, relaxed, relieved and, above all, knowing you got the most bang for your buck. We have scoured the city to find the hidden gems, new hot spots, and old standbys, all with one thing in common: they're the best of the best!

A Guide to our Guide

CRAVE Toronto is more than a guidebook. It's a savvy, quality-of-lifestyle book devoted entirely to the best local businesses owned by women. CRAVE Toronto will direct you to more than 100 local spots—top boutiques, spas, cafes, stylists, fitness studios, and more. And we'll introduce you to the inspired, dedicated women behind these exceptional enterprises, for whom creativity, quality, innovation, and customer service are paramount. Not only is CRAVE Toronto an intelligent guidebook for those wanting to know what's happening throughout town, it's a directory for those who value the contributions that spirited businesswomen make to our city.

Consumer Business Section
Consumer-driven entreprenesses, including boutiques, spas, and food.

Intelligentsia Section
Business-to-business entreprenesses, including coaching, marketing and public relations, photography, business consulting, and design services.

CRAVE Categories
ABODE - Home/interior design related goods and services.
ADORN - Jewellery-related goods and services.
CHILDREN'S - Baby, children, and mom-related goods and services.
CONNECT - Networking, media, technology, and event services.
DETAILS - Miscellaneous goods and services.
ENHANCE - Spa, salon, beauty, fitness studios, and personal trainers.
SIP SAVOUR - Food, drink, and caterers.
STYLE - Clothing, shoes, eyewear, handbags, stylists, etc.
PETS - Pet-related goods and services.

What do you CRAVE?
In business? In life?

"*People who have
integrity and a
desire to make
someone's world
better ... and
are ambitious
enough to do it.*"

Ali McEwen of Baby On Board Apparel

69 VINTAGE

1100 Queen St W, Toronto, 416.516.0669
1207 Bloor St W, Toronto, 416.516.1234
69vintage.com

Timeless. Free-spirited. Trendsetting.
"You've got to put it on to pull it off."—Kealan
69 Vintage is a style-driven brand with authentic vintage as the heart and soul
of the company. Over half a decade and two locations later, the trademark
of 69 Vintage remains one of originality, quality, and inspiration.

Kealan Sullivan

 Q and A

What are your most popular products or services?
Lots and lots of new product every week
and an ongoing customer "wish list" keeps
69 Vintage super fresh and personal.

People may be surprised to know...
I select every item by hand. I wash
everything (except the boots and furs!),
and I alter and repair ruined items to
create current and innovative styles.

What business mistake have you
made that you will not repeat?
I once gave someone (that I trusted) a large
sum of money without putting an agreement in
writing first. A very costly and important lesson.

What do you CRAVE? In business? In life?
Freedom, challenge, connection, and purpose.

AYALA RAITER
JEWELRY COUTURE

7787 Yonge St, Ste 205 (Second Floor), Thornhill, 647.293.7396
ayalaraiter.com, Twitter: @ayalaraiter, facebook.com/ayalaraiter

Eye-catching. Couture. Enhancing.
One-of-a-kind crafted art jewellery for the woman who is ahead of the
curve. Natural jewellery that bolds the inner beauty of any woman and
complements her natural beauty. Jewellery that grabs attention.

Ayala Raiter
Jewelry Couture

Ayala Raiter

Q and A

What are your most popular products or services?
Uniquely designed jewellery pieces embedded
with individually selected precious gems,
Swarovski crystals, leather, fabric, and
other natural elements. My artistic ability
to bring together a signature fitting based
on each person's needs and lifestyle.

What or who inspired you to start your business?
Several years ago, I was drawn to a necklace
worn by a good friend. The simplicity of
that piece motivated me to challenge my
imagination and creativity: to fuse together
seemingly unrelated elements and arrive at a
balanced, expressive statement each time.

How do you spend your free time?
I love to spend time with my husband,
children, and good friends. I enjoy tasting
new foods, listening to a variety of
music, and reading inspiring books.

BABY ON BOARD APPAREL

Toronto, 416.829.2459
babyonboardapparel.com, Twitter: @bobabyali, facebook.com/babyonboardapparel

Fashionable. Canadian-made. Indulgent.
Baby On Board Apparel (BOBA) offers fashion-forward maternity apparel for fashionistas
with blossoming bellies. Started in 2009 as a maternity tee shirt company, BOBA will
dominate the world of fashion in 2010. The spring will showcase a unique collection
called 9 Months Thru, that will still be as chic as ever when the bun is out of the oven.

Ali McEwen

 Q and A

What are your most popular products or services?
The Celebration tee shirt collection offers
a variety of prints. At the moment my most
popular shirt is the UltraSound Tee. And how
can it not be, with its huge emotional appeal?

What or who inspired you to start your business?
1. My father, who is one of the most
entrepreneurial people I know, 2. My pregnant
sister, who is one of my biggest ambassadors,
and 3. The sweetest little girl I have ever
met, when I was in Cambodia in 2005.

What do you CRAVE? In business? In life?
I CRAVE storytellers; from a 5-year-old talking
about a day at school to an 80-year-old sharing
stories about the good old days. I love stories!
In business, I CRAVE people who have
integrity and a desire to make someone's world
better and are ambitious enough to do it.

Anna Tvinnereim and Rose Hill

What are your most popular products or services?
Healthy, seasonal, made-from-scratch soups and salads, delicious quiches, and authentic Swedish cinnamon buns.

What or who inspired you to start your business?
We were presented with an opportunity and realised that by combining our skills, we could really make a go of it.

Where is your favourite place to go with your girlfriends?
Exploring vibrant neighbourhoods for relaxation and inspiration.

What business mistake have you made that you will not repeat?
Not having the guts to commit to a plan that we believed in. As Anna says: "You can't sell what you don't have!"

BEACHES BAKE SHOP & CAFÉ

900 Kingston Rd, Toronto, 416.686.2391
Twitter: @beachesbakeshop, facebook.com/beachesbakeshop

Local. Friendly. Warm.
Beaches Bake Shop & Café is a place to meet old friends and make new ones while enjoying a nourishing, seasonal menu. Experience authentic Swedish fare as part of their everyday offering. The café is also helping educate the next generation in healthy eating with their Taste Buddies Cooking Classes for kids. Catering is yet another service they offer.

Angela Panigas

Q and A

People may be surprised to know...
The Sultan's Tent & Café Moroc are
"where toronto celebrates," and we have
the best rack of lamb in the city!

What or who inspired you to
start your business?
My husband's idea to provide Toronto
with unique entertainment venues,
influenced by our experiences and
ideas gained through our travels.

Who is your role model or mentor?
The master, Walt Disney, who was
the leader in creating extraordinary
experiences and memories.

What business mistake have you
made that you will not repeat?
I do not believe there are any
mistakes, only solutions.

BERBER
RESTO.BAR.LOUNGE

49 Front St E, Toronto, 416.860.9000
berberlounge.ca, Twitter: @berberlounge

THE SULTAN'S TENT
& CAFÉ MOROC

49 Front St E, Toronto, 416.961.0601
thesultanstent.com, Twitter: @thesultanstent

Unique. Exotic. Entertaining.
The Sultan's Tent transports guests into an oasis of plush divans and lantern-lit tents. Enjoy a delectable French-Moroccan feast while admiring the belly dancer's charms. Jewel-tone fabrics and cushions create colourful, intimate spaces perfect for celebrations. The journey continues at BerBer Lounge, where guests savour tantalizing cocktails while dancing the night away to the beat of our DJ.

Photos by KBT PHOTOGRAPHY

BERGO DESIGNS

55 Mill St, Building 47a, Toronto, 416.861.1821
bergo.ca

CORKTOWN DESIGNS

55 Mill St, Building 59-102, Toronto, 416.861.3020
corktowndesigns.com

Unique. Inspiring. Original.
Bergo Designs is a gallery of industrial designs that is unique, modern, and stylish.
No knockoffs here! Bergo features award-winning designs from around the world,
including: Alessi, Georg Jensen, Stelton, Menu, Umbra, and Koziol among others.
You'll find a wide range of designs for jewellery, watches, gifts, housewares, and
Canadian-made furniture, not to mention a gift for every age and budget.

Photos by Photography

'GOLDFISH' EGGCUP
Design: Stefano Giovannoni, Rumiko
Takeda for Alessi
Material: hand decorated first bone china
$44

Robyn Berman

 Q and A

What are your most popular products or services?
Ethenol stainless steel fireplaces, lucite
vases, The Ex knife block, Govino plastic
wine glasses, Kikkerland head scratchers,
Chilewich placemats and floor rugs, Peugot
wine decanters, and Bodum glassware.

People may be surprised to know...
That Bergo Designs is a sole-proprietorship,
and that I travel constantly around the world to
hand-pick each item that is sold in the store.

What or who inspired you to start your business?
My husband. He strongly encouraged
me to expand Corktown Designs, my first
shop, which offers primarily handmade
jewellery. I came up with Bergo and decided
to keep them as two separate stores.

What is your indulgence?
Soma chocolate.

Q and A

What are your most popular
products or services?
Doggie treats, dog cakes,
healthy food, and gifts.

People may be surprised to know...
Our treats are actually for dogs. They easily
look as though you can eat them yourself!

Where is your favourite place to
go with your girlfriends?
A good old-fashioned night out on the town!

What do you CRAVE? In business? In life?
To be able to franchise my business, find the
balance to enjoy life, and travel the world.

What or who inspired you to
start your business?
Our Great Dane, Trixie, who is
now nearly 8 years old!

Jackie Krovblit

BIG DOG BAKERY

2014 Queen St E, Toronto, 416.551.0234
bigdogbakery.com, facebook.com/bigdogbakeryshop

Lovely. Holistic. Fun.
Big Dog Bakery is Toronto's only real dog bakery, specializing in holistic, human-grade treats and food mainly for dogs. Almost all of the cookies, muffins, cakes, and savoury snacks in the bakery cases are handmade right in the store. They proudly offer all-Canadian foods, including raw and a variety of grain- and wheat-free bulk treats. The boutique has many unique items from toys and chews to coats and beds—and they even cater to kitties!

Joanne Lowe

What or who inspired you to start your business?
It was an organic, natural growth of an idea, evolving out of wanting to be my own boss, doing something that I loved, and using my creativity.

What is your indulgence?
One-of-a-kind jewellery with natural, organic gemstones and, of course, cashmere.

Where is your favourite place to go with your girlfriends?
Taking turns creating fabulous dinners in our own homes.

What do you CRAVE? In business? In life?
Time. More time to just be, without obligations—mmmm, yes, time and laughter. Yes, more laughter.

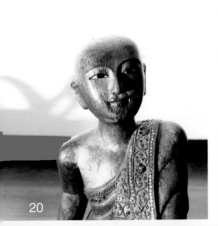

THE BIG STRETCH YOGA CENTRE

1560 Bayview Ave, Ste 303, Toronto, 416.486.4448
bigstretchyoga.com

Joyful. Inspired. Creative.
Breathe, stretch, relax. A small, intimate yoga centre that opened its doors in 1999,
The Big Stretch is a warm, welcoming space that offers Hatha yoga classes to
all age groups. With candles, inspiring music, and a small group of instructors,
classes are tailored to and inspired by the dynamics of the group attending.
The Big Stretch also offers corporate yoga, workshops, and retreats.

BIKO JEWELLERY

Toronto, 416.895.1071
bikodesigns.ca

Timeless. Cool. Chic.
Biko is a "vintage meets modern" jewellery brand possessing a natural, time-worn look with a twist of *au courant*. Designer Corrine Anestopoulos mixes the curious with the contemporary, combining semi-precious stones with raw metals such as brass, and integrating gold, crystal, pearl and lucite into her original, timeless accessories. The result is an irregular beauty that can be small and precious, or bold and freeform.

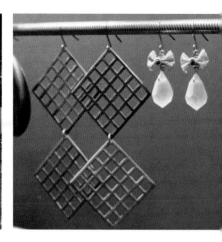

Corrine Anestopoulos

 Q and A

What are your most popular products or services?
Kaleidoscope, Telescope, Charlie magnifier
necklaces—they actually work! Clusters,
lockets, movement necklaces—quirky cool.
Leafdrops, vintage glam earrings—sweet, edgy.

People may be surprised to know...
Biko is green. Most materials used are vintage,
dead stock, and re-purposed. All jewellery
is handmade locally in Toronto, with love.

Who is your role model or mentor?
My mom. She is always eager to assist
the research and design process, and
her spirited energy is contagious.

How do you spend your free time?
Travelling for inspiration, walking in
the sunshine, supporting independent
businesses, and appreciating good design.

Tara **Clark** and Melanie **Groom**
(franchise partners)

What are your most popular products or services?
Blo's signature "blo outs" and products, like freshman (whipped crème conditioner), knockout (ultimate shine spray), and player (style-to-burn paste)!

What or who inspired you to start your business?
We have been best friends for more than 10 years and have always aspired to own and run a business together.

Who is your role model or mentor?
Mel: My parents are absolutely my role models. They encouraged me to be independent and strive for what I want. Tara: My younger sister has always excelled at sales and communication. I have a high respect for her.

What is your indulgence?
Both of us heart red wine and chocolate!

BLO BLOW DRY BAR

Yonge Street: 2594 Yonge St, Toronto, 416.440.4256
Four Seasons Toronto: 21 Ave Rd, Toronto, 416.920.2256
Oakville: 107 Thomas St, Oakville, 905.845.2568
King Street West: 626 King St W, Ste 102, Toronto, 416.703.1256
Bloor West Village: 2195 Bloor St W, Toronto, 416.766.4400
blomedry.com, Twitter: @bloheartsyou, facebook.com/bloheartsyou

Affordable. Convenient. Luxurious.
Blo is a blow dry bar. Scissors are verboten. Dye, ditto. For around $30, in about 30 minutes, get a wash and blow out style. No cuts, no colour: just WASH BLOW GO. Clients—also known as "hair cadets"—choose from seven styles featured in the blo hair menu, from the sexy razor-straight "Executive Sweet" to the rocker-chick inspired "Sex, Hugs, and Rock & Roll."

BLOSSOM BATH & BODY

Blossom Bath & Body: 205 Main St, Unionville, 905.479.8311
Blossom Bath & Body: Toronto Dominion Centre, 66 Wellington St W, Concourse Level, 416.364.8311
Blossom Lounge: 157 Main St, Unionville, 905.479.8355
blossomlounge.com, Twitter: @blossomlounge, facebook.com/blossomlounge

Fresh. Unique. Essential.
Blossom Bath & Body is a unique retail experience providing consumers with exclusive bath, body, cosmetic, and fragrance lines that are hard to find in the Canadian marketplace. First launched online in 2004, Blossom has since grown to brick-and-mortar locations in the greater Toronto area, focusing on independent product lines created by young, female entrepreneurs.

$\mathcal{Q}$ and $\mathcal{A}$

Shauna Podruzny

People may be surprised to know...
I became pregnant only six months into launching my business, and my son started coming to work with me when he was two days old. As demanding as it was at the time, it has never overwhelmed me, and I have always managed to find a way to make it work.

What or who inspired you to start your business?
The frustration at the time of not having any good retailers carrying small, independent, international lines that I would read about in magazines.

Who is your role model or mentor?
I look up to all women entrepreneurs. I am always motivated and inspired by other women who strive to succeed in the marketplace.

How do you spend your free time?
I try to spend almost all of my free time with my son and husband, whether it's going to the zoo or just hanging out in the neighbourhood. It's so good to unwind with the ones that love you the most!

27

BLUEBIRD HANDMADE

986 Bathurst St, Toronto, 416.535.3232
bluebirdhandmade.com

Natural. Inspirational. Modern.
Bluebird Handmade is a retail shop in the Annex that carries an array of handmade ceramics, stationery, print scarves, jewellery, bags, felt art, natural handwork supplies, and just plain oddities that have been sourced from Toronto and around the world. Bluebird is a pleasure to behold even before entering the store. The inventive window displays convey a feeling that you are entering something worthy of magic. Bluebird also offers creative birthday parties and felting workshops.

Photos by KBT PHOTOGRAPHY

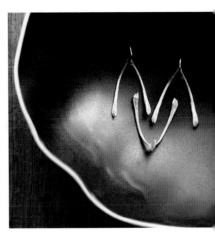

Crystal Silden

 Q and A

What are your most popular products or services?
Felted creatures by little m inventions, wool felt,
unusual dolls and softies, jewellery, porcelain
hold jars, felting workshops, and parties.

Who is your role model or mentor?
My father taught me: Where
there is will, there is way.

What do you CRAVE? In business? In life?
Creating, finding originality, and seeing my
children grow up and discover who they are.

What is your indulgence?
I buy too many books and eat out
at restaurants too much.

Where is your favourite place to
go with your girlfriends?
Dinners, art shows, or movies.

What or who inspired you to start your business?

"*I wanted a life where creativity wasn't edited. I wanted to run with ideas and push design boundaries.*"

Katina Constantinou of Sugar

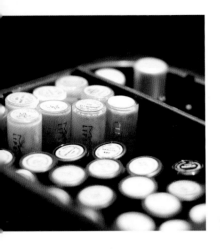

Stephanie Daga

 Q and A

What are your most popular products or services?
Definitely bridal beauty services and The Beauty Board events. Women love getting primped and pampered ... and swag bags!

What do you CRAVE? In business? In life?
I crave success, strong and supportive relationships, and a clean home. Yes, a clean home ... I work better when the house is tidy.

People may be surprised to know...
That I took a leap of faith and quit my full-time job without really knowing where BlushPretty would go ... without a business plan.

What is your indulgence?
Purses. Anyone who knows me knows about my passion for purses. I'm also a sucker for Dr. Pepper.

BLUSHPRETTY: MAKEUP & HAIR ARTISTRY AND BLUSHPRETTY.COM

Toronto, 416.727.1754
blushpretty.com, Twitter: @blushpretty, facebook.com/BlushPrettyTheBlushBoutique

Fresh. Beautiful. Fun.
BlushPretty: Makeup & Hair Artistry provides makeup and hair services for bridal, personal, and corporate clients, and editorial photography in the GTA. BlushPretty.com is *the* online resource for women seeking beauty insight and great tips. The site provides friendly guidance and a look at the life of a beauty expert. BlushPretty's mantra is, "Beauty is easy!"

33

BODY BLITZ
HEALTH BY WATER

471 Adelaide St W, Toronto, 416.364.0400
bodyblitzspa.com, Twitter: @bodyblitzspa, facebook.com/bodyblitzspa

Modern. Urban. Oasis.
Body blitz is a women's spa that puts a modern twist on ancient restorative water practices.
Situated in an 11,000 square-foot warehouse in the heart of Toronto, body blitz boasts a
38-foot Dead Sea salt pool with 24 hydrotherapy jets, a hot green tea pool, a cold plunge
pool, aromatherapy steam, an infrared sauna, and massage, face, and body treatments.

Photos by Jennifer Klementti Photography

Rena and Laura Polley

Q and A

What are your most popular products or services?
Therapeutic water circuit, scrub, and
mud treatments and our incredible
argan oil face serum.

What or who inspired you to start your business?
Visiting thermal spas in Europe and
Asia and realising there was a market
for this concept in Toronto.

What business mistake have you
made that you will not repeat?
Not having the financing firmly in
place before the cement was.

What do you CRAVE? In business? In life?
Bankers who realise that businesses owned by
women are a good investment. And, of course,
laughter, creativity, and a few nice clothes.

Sandra Tarantino

Q and A

What are your most popular products or services?
Our art workshops are a favourite, especially silk screening and wheel throwing. Lots of handmade gifts, including Julie Moon poppy pins, Avril Loreti napkins, Yasmine Louis and Ross Bonfanti apparel, and more.

People may be surprised to know...
They can learn to be creative. Our classes are fun and relaxed, so it's easy to learn how to D.I.Y.

What or who inspired you to start your business?
My love of art and teaching have always existed since I was a child. I've been planning to do this forever.

What do you CRAVE? In business? In life?
Calmness and happiness ... always.

C1 ART SPACE:
ART SHOP, ART SCHOOL

C1 art space: 44 Ossington Ave, Toronto, 416.538.7999
AWOL Gallery and Studios: 76 Ossington Ave, Toronto, 416.535.5637
c1artspace.com, awolgallery.com

Quirky. Humourous. Fun.
C1 art space, open since November 2004, is a project developed by artist/teacher Sandra Tarantino and her husband, artist Ross Bonfanti. C1 art space houses a variety of activities from art shop to art school, with the aim of being a welcoming community environment. The art shop showcases an assortment of handmade Canadian fine crafts, gift items, artist apparel and more.

Diane Iannuzziello

What are your most popular products or services?
Diplomas, corporate awards and events, weddings, bar/bat mitzvahs, addressed envelopes, place cards, lessons, and my book and kit.

People may be surprised to know...
Hand-done calligraphy is not a dying art. In this high-tech world, calligraphy has come full circle and is in demand now more than ever.

How do you spend your free time?
Reading, golfing, and enjoying nature while taking a break from city life.

What is your indulgence?
I enjoy good humour and I love to laugh.

What business mistake have you made that you will not repeat?
Giving a quote over the phone.

CALLIGRAPHY BY DIANE

260 King St E, Ste A 408, Toronto, 416.703.4977
calligraphybydiane.com, Twitter: @calligraphybydi

Perfect. Reliable. Beautiful.
Diane Iannuzziello, is a perfectionist who insists all of her work far exceeds expectations. It is that level of service that has made her the most sought-after calligrapher. She can do any lettering style in any language for your project. With more than 30 years of professional experience, Calligraphy by Diane offers a 100 percent guarantee for perfectly and beautifully done calligraphy.

CAROL REED INTERIOR DESIGN INC.

Toronto, 416.259.4020
carolreeddesign.com, thedesignshop.ca, Twitter: @carolreeddesign

Expert. Innovative. Intuitive.
Carol Reed Interior Design is a full-service design firm specializing in private, residential renovation projects. With more than 16 years of experience, Carol's portfolio includes chic urban condos and elegant family homes. Recognized for her clean, modern approach to traditionally inspired interiors, Carol has worked for a top-rated HGTV show and her work has been featured in major publications.

Carol Reed

People may be surprised to know...
Hiring an interior designer will save you money!

What or who inspired you to start your business?
After a 10-year career in commercial design,
undertaking a complete gut and renovation of
my own home inspired me to pursue my own
practice specializing in residential design projects.

What business mistake have you
made that you will not repeat?
In a fee-based business, underestimating
my time on projects and giving my time
and services away without compensation
is the worst mistake I could make.

What do you CRAVE? In business? In life?
Access to quality products that are well designed
and offer great style at affordable prices. More
online retailers who ship to Canada. More time to
travel and more time to design my own home!

THE CASHMERE SHOP

24 Bellair St, Toronto, 416.925.0831
thecashmereshop.com, Twitter: @alycashmere

Elegant. Cosy. Authentic.
The Cashmere Shop is Toronto's original specialty shop for cashmere. In business for more than 17 years, they use only the highest quality cashmere yarn. Garments are exclusively designed and knitted for this boutique.

Photos by IrinaPhotography

Alison Currie

 Q and A

What are your most popular products or services?
Wraps are our most popular and versatile
item. Every woman should own one!

People may be surprised to know...
We have sweaters for everyone,
ages 1 month to 99 years old.

What or who inspired you to start your business?
In 2003, I took over my family business.
It's been an amazing experience.

Who is your role model or mentor?
Retail maven Shirley Dawe. She has
taught me to think BIG and take risks.

What is your indulgence?
Chocolate chip cookies from Wagamama,
a bakery close to my house. They are
the most delicious cookies ever!

Teresa Wiwchar

Q and A

What are your most popular
products or services?
Painted vintage furniture, romantic
lighting, and feel-good gifts.

People may be surprised to know...
I am a competitive water skier in slalom
and own a Harley-Davidson.

Who is your role model or mentor?
My husband. He took me to a flea market
for our first date. He's helped train my
eye and taught me how to haggle.

What business mistake have you
made that you will not repeat?
Not researching the city where I opened
a second location well enough, and
having to close it 11 months later.

CHATELET

717 Queen St W, Toronto, 416.603.2278
2207 Queen St E, Toronto, 416.698.2207
chatelethome.com, facebook.com/chatelethome

CHATELET KIDS

719 Queen St W, Toronto, 416.603.2278

Whimsical. Girly. Glamourous.
Chatelet and Chatelet Kids, brain children of Teresa Wiwchar, are side-by-side boutiques
in Toronto's Queen Street West district. On offer are Teresa's hand-picked vintage furniture
pieces that have been lovingly painted and distressed. More than 100 chandeliers adorn
the ceiling, and perfect gift items and accessories grace every available surface.

Photos by IrinaPhotography

Q and A

Andrea Pahn

What are your most popular products or services?
All of our polishes are popular, but Brazen Hussy, Hot Slut ,and Raunchy Bitch have turned out to be our biggest sellers. I guess women are getting the "show your true colours" joke!

Who is your role model or mentor?
My mother, as she is a good old girl, and even in tough times she finds a way to laugh.

How do you spend your free time?
Shopping, skiing, mountain biking with my kids, and misbehaving with my friends.

What do you CRAVE? In business? In life?
In business, I crave total world domination! In life, I would like my family to remain as close as we are right now—forever. Not too much to ask, right?

Remember that a piece of chocolate cake can't get you pregnant

CHEEKY MONKEY COSMETICS

Toronto, 905.299.1917
cheekymonkeycosmetics.com, Twitter: @cheekymonkeycos, facebook.com/cheekymonkeycosmetics

Edgy. Quality. Humourous.
Cheeky Monkey Cosmetics helps bring some fun back into women's stressful lives.
Cheeky Monkey has the highest quality nail polishes that not only make a woman's
hands look fabulous but the names will also bring a smile to her face. Visit online to get
some dynamite drink recipes and read some fun silliness that will brighten your day.

CITRA HAIR STUDIO

393 Danforth Ave, 2nd Floor, Toronto, 416.778.9585
citrahairstudio.com

Attentive. Conscientious. Diverse.
Citra, through the efforts of four determined women and despite many trials,
has arrived. Walk through the door, and you'll see both new and familiar faces.
Sporting a fresh new look and philosophy, the Citra team is excited to take on
the challenges of servicing its vibrant, energetic, and green community.

Photos by KBT PHOTOGRAPHY

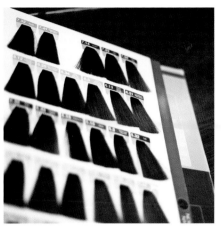

Darylene Campbell, Ashley Davie, Angie Georgopoulos, and Mandye Bronson

Q and A

What are your most popular products or services?
Kevin Murphy, Purology and L'Oreal
Professional Colour, as well as a thorough
consultation with every service.

People may be surprised to know...
We are owner operated, and involved
with Green Circle Salons to have a
positive impact on the environment.

What business mistake have you
made that you will not repeat?
Putting our garbage out on the wrong day,
and getting a ticket ($425). So rest assured,
we'll always be on point with garbage day.

How do you spend your free time?
Mandye: Wining and dining.
Angie: Poker night with wine.
Ashley: Reading, dating, and listening to music.
Darylene: With family and friends.

Annette Hansen

Q and A

What are your most popular products or services?
Adult and kid pottery lessons. The gallery is an inspiration and leads to discussions about art.

What or who inspired you to start your business?
Soul searching, the support of my family, and the opportunity to buy a pottery studio and revamp it into a gallery/studio. It was a dream-come-true.

How do you spend your free time?
Besides spending time with my family and friends, I escape in a good book or watch old black-and-white movies.

What is your indulgence?
Shoes, books, chocolate, a good cup of Earl Grey tea or fabulous coffee, buying art.

COBALT GALLERY AND CLAY STUDIO

870a Kingston Rd, Toronto, 416.694.0156
cobaltgallery.ca

Creative. Unique. Inspiring.
COBALT GALLERY is an intimate and casual gallery space available for emerging and established artists to rent and present solo or group exhibitions. The gallery promotes quality art and fine craft. COBALT features Annette Hansen's own unique style of functional and decorative ceramics and also offers pottery lessons for adults and kids.

Diana Howson

Q and A

People may be surprised to know...
The quest for the perfect hand bag, lipstick, or red high heels may not solve world hunger, but humanitarians and philanthropists can have more than one cause at a time.

What or who inspired you to start your business?
The clock—it was ticking.

What business mistake have you made that you will not repeat?
Hanging on too long or staying too long at something when it's time to let go, move on, and move forward.

Where is your favourite place to go with your girlfriends?
In the summer, I like the patio at Karen's Wine Bar, as well as my own patio and garden for entertaining friends and family at home.

COCO&JULES BOUTIQUE LTD.

1013 Yonge St, Toronto, 416.921.8222
Twitter: @cocoandjules

Feminine. Spirited. Chic.
Coco&Jules Boutique serves up jewellery and accessories with sweetness and sass. With an ultra-fem vibe and vintage decor, it features Parisian-sourced scarves, Brit-chic bags, vintage-inspired baubles and sparkles, wraps and shawls, and jewellery from international and Canadian designers. Whimsical and very girly, with a certain *je ne sais quoi*, and enough edge for the savvy fashionista.

CONCEPTION DESIGN SOLUTIONS

Toronto, 647.295.2512
conceptiondesign.ca, Twitter: @conceptn_design, facebook.com/conceptiondesign

Refined. Dependable. Creative.
A design is nothing without the "conception" of ideas, creative talent, and design excellence!
Behind conception design solutions is designer, thinker, and photographer Richelle Dayle
Chapman, who provides clients with graphic solutions that work! With a passion for art and a
career in design, Richelle discovered her love for photography through travelling around the
world and capturing snapshots in an attempt to freeze moments and places in a single image.

Q and A

What are your most popular products or services?
My graphic design services and visual
solutions. Merging photography with
design, I create calendars with theme-
inspired photographs, which are popular.

People may be surprised to know...
I have an obsession with collecting anything
and everything visually pleasing—contributing
to my overflowing printed ephemera collection.

What or who inspired you to start your business?
The love I have for the arts, design, typography,
and photography, and my desire to compose,
capture, and create something in a unique way,
whether it be a visual design or photograph.

What is your indulgence?
I have a few! Pens, pencils, paper, dark
chocolate, a good glass of red wine,
and finding new places to go, locally or
abroad. Travel, travel, and more travel!

Richelle Dayle Chapman

What business mistake
have you made that
you will not repeat?

" *Viewing mistakes
as negative.* "

Jennifer Neill/Valerie Neill of JUDY BLACK !

CONTINUUM
MODERN VINTAGE

707 Pape Ave, Toronto, 416.778.1200
continuummodernvintage.ca

Eclectic. Inspiring. Unique.
Continuum Modern Vintage provides constantly changing vignettes of home decor items for every room in the house—from antique to modern, from furniture to glassware, from jewellery to vintage clothing—as well as custom design services for draperies, headboards, slipcovers, re-upholstering, etc. Continuum Modern Vintage gives life to things old and new. Design never stops at Continuum Modern Vintage.

Daina Liepa

Q and A

What are your most popular products or services?
The most popular products are those that are
unusual or unique. The most popular services
are custom draperies and slipcovers.

People may be surprised to know...
That the inventory changes every day. Once I
sell a piece, it's gone and has to be replaced
with something completely different.

What or who inspired you to start your business?
It's an idea I've been developing for a
few years: giving older pieces of furniture
a new life. It grew from there.

Where is your favourite place to
go with your girlfriends?
Drinking wine in my backyard in the
summer while pretending we're in Italy.

CRE8IVE INVITATIONS

Toronto, 416.550.1506
cre8iveinvitations.com

Distinctive. Elegant. Luxurious.
Cre8ive Invitations offers custom invitations and stationery for all occasions. With stylish elegance, stunning paper, and attention to every detail, each invitation is created by hand. Adorned with luxurious embellishments, such as Swarovski crystals, pearls, ribbons, or buckles, each invitation is like receiving a gift in the mail. Their philosophy: The event begins the moment your guest opens the invitation. Set it in motion and ignite excitement!

Patricia Figueira

Q and A

What are your most popular products or services?
Wedding stationery, from the custom invitation
to the order of service, menus, escort and/or
seating cards, favour tags, thank you cards, etc.

People may be surprised to know...
That great design can be affordable.

What or who inspired you to start your business?
Friends and family. They recognized the passion
I have for great design and all things paper.

How do you spend your free time?
By the lake with my family, a coffee, and a
big comfy lawn chair—mesmerized by the
tranquility. Life tends to slow down by the lake.

What do you CRAVE? In business? In life?
I crave the new, the unexpected. I crave
the look on my clients' faces when they
see their invitation for the first time.

DANCEOLOGY

171 E Liberty St, Unit 109, Toronto, 416.588.0111
danceology.org, Twitter: @danceologyorg, facebook.com/danceology

Urban. Social. Fun
Danceology seeks to enhance people's lives and the quality of their relationships by making ballroom dance easy and fun. They are dedicated to providing the ultimate social dance experience for each participant, giving the utmost attention to teaching and learning in their studio. The teaching style is encouraging and inspiring while the teaching technique is knowledgeable and designed to develop grace, harmony, poise, connection, enjoyment, confidence, and creativity.

Photos by DSF Imaging

Marla Silva

Q and A

What are your most popular products or services?
We are the first and only ballroom and
Latin social dance studio that has a
membership option which gives students
the opportunity to spend $99 a month for
unlimited dance, Pilates, and yoga classes.

People may be surprised to know...
Ballroom and Latin dancing has become a
social hobby for the younger generation.

What or who inspired you to start your business?
Giving the gift of dance is the most rewarding
experience; creating an environment where
you can enhance people's lives through dance
is the greatest inspiration I can ever ask for.

Who is your role model or mentor?
My role model is my mother.

DISTILL

55 Mill St, Building #47, Toronto, 416.304.0033
distillgallery.com

Creative. Eclectic. Canadian.
Established in 2003, distill shows the individual handmade works of more than 160 emerging
Canadian artists, craftspeople, designers contributing to contemporary material and visual culture.

 Q and A

Allison Skinner

What are your most popular products or services?
That is difficult to answer. distill's eclectic mix
is ever-changing since handmade work is
always unique and evolving. Jeweller Leslie
Jones' resin TTC and Toronto stuff bracelets
are always in demand, as is just about any
clothing designed by Susan Harris.

What or who inspired you to start your business?
Originally I opened distill with my best friend,
Kelly. We cooked up the concept during a road
trip from Halifax to Charlottetown in search
of a good beach. My area of interest was fine
craft, her expertise was in home decor, and
we both loved fashion. It seemed logical to
us that all elements could be combined.

How do you spend your free time?
I enjoy time spent with my husband, Robert,
walking our dog, Mingus, creating ceramics,
playing tennis, watching movies, and eating
and drinking with friends or family.

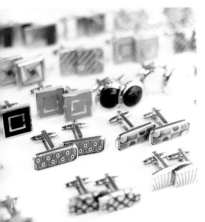

Laura Furtado

 Q and A

What are your most popular
products or services?
Strip to Fit classes, bachelorette party
bookings, and private dance lessons.

Who is your role model or mentor?
I admire Leanne Grechulk, founder
of HealthyGirl. She has been an
inspiration, supporter, and friend.

What is your indulgence?
Chocolate! I have a sweet tooth.

Where is your favourite place to
go with your girlfriends?
On the dance floor!

What do you CRAVE? In business? In life?
Being challenged in business
and inspired in life.

DIVAGIRL INC.

Toronto, 416.580.0611
divagirl-inc.com, Twitter: @divagirlfitness.com, facebook.com/divagirlfitness

Sexy. Flirty. Fun.
DivaGirl Inc. is an online female community dedicated to helping women get fit, have fun, and feel sexy! DivaGirl Fitness is an online source of various sexy dance and fitness-based classes and workshops hosted in your area. DivaGirl Entertainment is a premium dance entertainment company, consisting of professional, high-energy dancers and instructors, who entertain at Diva events and parties. DivaGirl Beauty is a one-stop shop for premier spa services and products to enhance special Diva occasions, parties, and events!

Photos by Jennifer Klementti Photography

DR | STEPHANIE

47 Stewart St, Toronto, 647.346.2281
drstephanie.ca, Twitter: @dr_stephanie

Passionate. Focused. Effective.
Dr. Stephanie is a big-hearted, energetic, and passionate healer. With a background in neuroscience and psychology, she understands how physical injury can, if left untreated, fully integrate into the body. Dr. Stephanie specializes in whole body wellness, including chiropractic treatments, cosmetic, cellulite, traditional acupuncture, orthotic therapy, and fitness.

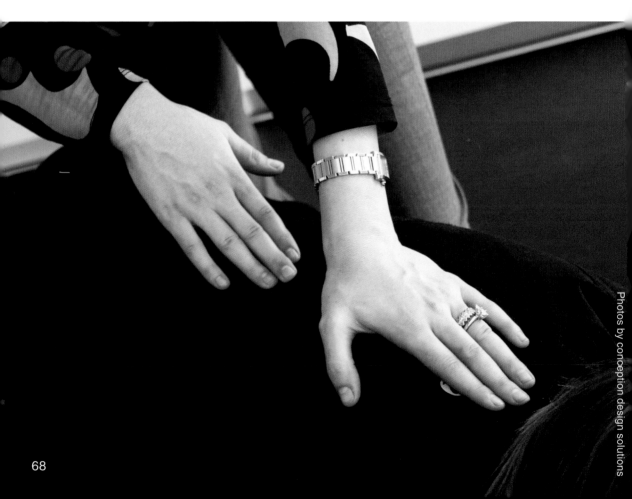

Photos by conception design solutions

Dr. Stephanie

$\mathcal{Q}$ and $\mathcal{A}$

What are your most popular products or services?
Chiropractic and acupuncture treatments,
custom orthotics for shoes, including stilettos
and heels, and weight-loss supplements.

People may be surprised to know...
I am trained in cosmetic and cellulite
acupuncture, and, yes, you can get great
support in your stilettos with my orthotics!

What or who inspired you to start your business?
The over-arching desire to help fabulous people
live their best lives and to promote health,
fitness, and healing from the inside out.

Who is your role model or mentor?
Michelle Obama. She is the perfect blend
of career woman, wife, and loving mother:
simultaneously feminine and strong.

Susan Drysdale

 Q and A

What are your most popular
products or services?
Jewellery, funny greeting cards and magnets,
bags and totes, journals, and stationery.

People may be surprised to know...
I grew up on a dairy farm in rural Ontario.

What or who inspired you to
start your business?
Ever since I was young, I just loved
shopping and wanted to live in the
city and have a store of my own.

Where is your favourite place to
go with your girlfriends?
For pints at one of the city's many great pubs.

What do you CRAVE? In business? In life?
To travel to the great cities of the world. I've
been to a few, but the list is still very long.

DRYSDALE & CO.

107 Danforth Ave, Toronto, 416.484.8592
drysdaleandco.com, Twitter: @drysdaleandco, facebook.com/drysdaleandco

Quirky. Colourful. Hip.
DRYSDALE & CO. is an eclectic gift, accessory, and jewellery boutique located on Danforth
Avenue in Toronto's Riverdale neighbourhood. Store owner Susan Drysdale and her staff search
the world for practical everyday items with a twist, focusing on items with beautiful design, strong
colours, and a bold sense of personality: the kind of goods people just love to give and receive.

Photos by KBT PHOTOGRAPHY

EKO JEWELLERY

288 Queen St W Toronto, 416.593.0776
2611 Yonge St, Toronto, 416.545.0776
ekojewellery.com

Fashionable. Inspirational. Artistic.
Eko is a unique shop that carries highly designed jewellery by contemporary
designers from all over the world. It offers Toronto's fashionistas
pieces that provoke and promote jewellery as wearable art.

Photos by conception design solutions except this page by Eric Lau

Mina Yoon

 Q and A

What or who inspired you to start your business?
My dad, who taught me: "the will
to do, the soul to dare."

How do you spend your free time?
Walking around the city looking for
inspiration, and having lunch with friends.

What is your indulgence?
Spending a day without phone calls.

Where is your favourite place to
go with your girlfriends?
Terroni's restaurant.

What do you CRAVE? In business? In life?
In business, stability, and continual creative
innovations. In life, contentment.

ELLA MINNOW CHILDREN'S BOOKSTORE

1915 Queen St E, Toronto, 416.698.2665
ellaminnow.ca, facebook.com/ella.minnow.books

Inspiring. Engaging. Nurturing.
Ella Minnow Children's Bookstore is all about love for children and books. Kids get to experience the right book at the right time, from baby's first cuddle with a book, through childhood growth and transitions, to teens and young adults finding their way with inspiration. Reading makes the world a bigger, better place for all of us!

Heather Kuipers

Q and A

What are your most popular products or services?
Books! Though we have lots of clever
games, puzzles, and toys, too.

People may be surprised to know...
Ella Minnow is home to two friendly
rabbits who share our enthusiasm for
books—they love to chew on them.

What or who inspired you to start your business?
My passion to share Anne, Harry, Emily,
Winnie, Fern, Fiver, Wilbur, and so
many others with my community.

What business mistake have you
made that you will not repeat?
We must always consider the products
we offer with child-like eyes. What looks
clever to an adult doesn't always appeal
to children, and our focus is children.

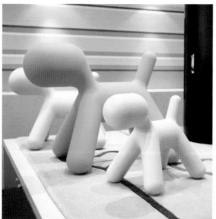

Suzanne O'Leary

Q and A

What or who inspired you to
start your business?
My son—especially after living in
the Netherlands and being exposed
to beautiful European designs.

Who is your role model or mentor?
Hillary Clinton for representing intelligence,
liberty and feminine power. She does
not take a backseat to any men.

What business mistake have you
made that you will not repeat?
Expecting more supportive relationships.

What is your indulgence?
Luxury clothing and accessories
and design magazines.

What do you CRAVE? In business? In life?
Civility in business. Knowledge in life.

ELLA+ELLIOT

188 Strachan Ave, Toronto, 416.850.7890
ellaandelliot.com, Twitter: @ellaandelliot

Modern. Timeless. Sustainable.
Ella+elliot offers the best and the largest selection of modern design for babies and kids in
Canada. Its unique approach to showcasing products with simple lines, multiple functions, and
sustainablility makes it easy for parents to choose products that will integrate perfectly in their
homes. Since its opening in 2007, ella+elliot has expanded to a second floor and online.

Photos by Jennifer Klementti Photography

Eren and Jais Fernandez with Chef Mali Fernandez

What are your most popular
products or services?
Tapas, flamenco shows, and paella.

People may be surprised to know...
Originally, tapas were slices of bread meant
to keep fruit flies away from wine glasses.

Who is your role model or mentor?
El Buli, the best restaurant in Spain.

What business mistake have you
made that you will not repeat?
Not having a bar for patrons, since the bar
Café Madrid is just opening this year.

What do you CRAVE? In business? In life?
Fulfilling life by doing what we love. Providing
opportunities for women when possible.

EMBRUJO FLAMENCO TAPAS RESTAURANT & CAFÉ MADRID BAR

97 Danforth Ave, Toronto, 416.778.0007
embrujoflamenco.com, Twitter: @embrujotapasbar

Welcoming. Trendy. Delicious.
Embrujo Flamenco specializes in the regional cuisines of Spain. The restaurant is cosy, warm, and welcoming. Tapas are "sharing" dishes. Spanish cuisine celebrates centuries of traditional cooking and hundreds of regional recipes based on natural ingredients such as olive oil, seafood, vegetables, game, veal, ham, and sausages.

Erica Swanson

Q and A

What are your most popular
products or services?
My virtual interior design services by far
... stylish solutions that are respectful
of time and budget while offering a
personalized sense of luxury.

Who is your role model or mentor?
Angela Scott, creator of Procrastenough
Coaching & Learning, for being a
shining light of inspiration and truth. And
Danielle LaPorte, founder of White Hot
Truth, for being so brazenly cool.

Where is your favourite place to
go with your girlfriends?
My dining room. I love providing a glamourous,
indulgent evening for the women I love most.

How do you spend your free time?
Learning everything I can. If I'm not
working toward one of my passions,
I feel restless and distracted.

ERICA SWANSON DESIGN

Toronto, 905.580.7008
ericaswansondesign.com, Twitter: @erica_swanson

Self. Not. Stuff.
Erica Swanson Design is focused on providing inspiring and accessible virtual interior design services to clients around the world, and creative design and lifestyle solutions to clients in the greater Toronto area. Style within reach, smart and savvy design solutions, and a non-intimidating approach: isn't it time your home and lifestyle reflected the essence of you?

What business mistake
have you made that
you will not repeat?

*" I used to worry too
much about the
market and restrict
my imagination
when creating
my product. I
found that when
I have faith in my
original creations,
customers will
come and buy. "*

Jacqueline Lo of Ruelo Patisserie

FEATHER FACTORY

1606 Queen St W, Toronto, 416.536.3391
featherfactory.com, facebook.com/featherfactory1

Ecofriendly. Creative. Dishy.
Feather Factory customers are greeted with light, colour, and texture, and often compliment
the Parisian feel. Rows of quilts, colourful duvet covers, cushions, and sumptuous high-thread-
count linens fill the boutique. Owners Cathy Bull, Martha Bull and Michelle Richardson have
sourced top, unique brands in bed linens, towels, fabrics, and wallpaper, and they make their
own superior down products. Their combined 85 years of linen experience is at your service.

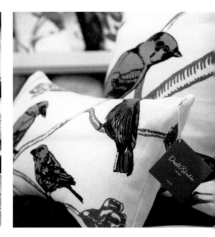

Martha Bull, Michele Richardson, and Cathy Bull

Q and A

People may be surprised to know...
We make our duvets, pillows, and featherbeds on the premises, and we made a pillow for Pope John Paul. We are all artists and feel that good bedroom design can often start with the art on your walls.

What or who inspired you to start your business?
Duvets that are innovative, eco-friendly and luxurious were the beginning (Martha pioneered duvets in Ontario), and a fabulous sisterhood inspired us to work together. Michelle is our adopted sister (she started working with Martha in the Eiderdown Shop 20 years ago).

What do you CRAVE? In business? In life?
Business success would include satellite Feather Factory boutiques across Canada, and in life, joy every day.

Katrin and Alina Maslenkova

Q and A

People may be surprised to know...
We are full-time students at ages 17 and 20
with a strong passion for entrepreneurship.

What or who inspired you to
start your business?
Our aunt and jeweller, Nadejda Petrova,
and her sparkling creations.

How do you spend your free time?
Exercising, playing sports, and spending
time with family and friends.

What do you CRAVE? In business? In life?
Happiness, turning our imaginative
creations into reality, and adding
sparkle to our customers' lives.

Who is your role model or mentor?
Our aunt, uncle, mom, and dad.

FEMM

Toronto, 647.213.2331
femm.ca, Twitter: @femmboutique

Elegant. Luxurious. Unique.
Femm Boutique offers a unique range of high-quality fashion and bridal jewellery, beautiful hand-painted silk scarves, and other accessories. The bracelets, earrings, and necklaces are handmade using crystallized Swarovski elements. In addition, some jewellery pieces contain freshwater pearls, gold-dipped real leaves and semi-precious stones. All products are uniquely 100% handmade in Europe and Canada. The jewellers are also available for custom work.

Photos by IrinaPhotography

Esther Ha and Jennifer Yang

What are your most popular
products or services?
Cakes and flowers, of course!

Who is your role model or mentor?
Our parents, who have worked so
hard, yet always made time for us.

What is your indulgence?
Travelling. It is so rare to have extended
time off, that when we do, we love to travel
to new places—we find this to be refreshing
and inspiring. We often come back with
a wealth of new ideas for our work.

What do you CRAVE? In business? In life?
A balance between work and life, since we
often allow our work to overtake our worlds.

What or who inspired you to
start your business?
Our hobbies, along with the encouragement
and trust of our family and friends.

FLOUR STUDIO
CAKE & FLORAL DESIGN

883 Eglinton Ave W, Toronto, 416.789.0222
flourstudio.com

Fresh. Delightful. Sweet.
Delight in goodies baked daily from scratch on premise. Local and exotic blooms are arranged with care alongside a well-edited selection of little gifts. Flour Studio also specializes in designing custom cakes and floral arrangements for all of life's celebrations, big and small.

FROCK & FROCK-HEAD

97 Roncesvalles Ave, Toronto, 416.516.1333
frock.ca

IMELDA

123 Roncesvalles Ave, Toronto, 647.344.1006
frock.ca

Quirky. Accessible. No-pressure.
Frock is one of those places where, if you take the time, you're sure to find something that suits your style and budget. It's a charming neighbourhood boutique with a diverse selection of distinctive women's fashions and accessories. Downstairs, frock-head offers a unique one-on-one hair-styling experience. A few doors up, Imelda has great shoes, boots, hats, and bags.

Frock

Frock

Imelda

Frock

Cathryn Dajka

 Q and A

What are your most popular products or services?
Accessories have a quick turn-over and our
Canadian clothing lines have a loyal fan base.

People may be surprised to know...
Roncesvalles Village has a lot to offer and it's
closer to downtown than you may think.

What or who inspired you to start your business?
I wanted to fill a niche in my neighbourhood,
and it's nice to be able to walk to work.

What is your indulgence?
All things vintage.

Where is your favourite place to
go with your girlfriends?
Time with the girls usually includes the
guys, usually at someone's home with good
food, good drink, and lots of laughs.

FUSS HAIR STUDIO

1093 Queen St E, Toronto, 416.469.0006
fusshairstudio.com

Sassy. Sustainable. Hip.
A quaint boutique salon located on Queen Street East in the heart of Leslieville. The eclectic music is a perfect backdrop for the friendly chatter and laughter of the stylists and clients in this intimate setting. Fuss is the perfect neighbourhood salon with just enough downtown edge to keep you and your hair in the loop. What could be better?

Photos by Tara McMullen

Stacey Lipstein and Kristin Rankin

 Q and A

People may be surprised to know...
We are a hip salon without the attitude. We are also a part of Green Circle Salons, which helps us reduce waste and our carbon footprint.

Who is your role model or mentor?
That is a hard one. Our mothers who taught us to be strong independent women, and never let anyone tell us no.

What is your indulgence?
The candies on our salon's front desk, they change seasonally. A girl's gotta eat.

Where is your favourite place to go with your girlfriends?
The local waterhole across the street, Strats. We go there after a long, hairy day.

Rebecca Nixon

 Q and A

What are your most popular products or services?
Our most popular products are dresses from our in-house label under the Girl Friday name. Because of the superior fit and comfort, Girl Friday dresses become instant favourites in clients' wardrobes and are perfect for all occasions.

How do you spend your free time?
I love to work out—anything from yoga to spinning to snowshoeing! I find it really improves my focus, and my mood, and it's a fantastic stress reliever.

What is your indulgence?
My indulgence is definitely travel. I love checking out boutiques and museums, and going to fantastic restaurants.

GIRL FRIDAY

776 College St, Toronto, 416.531.1036
740 Queen St W, Toronto, 416.364.2511
girlfridayclothing.com

Friendly. Fresh. Versatile.
Girl Friday is a women's clothing boutique featuring labels from around the world. The warm, inviting environment is filled with delectable pieces from a variety of price points, which offers shoppers on the tightest budget a new look. Girl Friday has two locations in Toronto and the in-house Girl Friday collection can be found in independent boutiques across Canada.

Photos by KBT PHOTOGRAPHY

Tiffany Pratt

Q and A

What are your most popular
products or services?
Birthday parties, special events, and
custom requests. Classes, special events,
workshops, parties, and an ever-producing
art studio are on the glittering menu always.

People may be surprised to know...
My entire apartment is white!

What business mistake have you
made that you will not repeat?
Not being tough enough. Sometimes
it is best to say no!

Where is your favourite place to
go with your girlfriends?
It is not the place, it is my friends. They
make any place my favourite.

What is your indulgence?
Oh Henry! chocolate bars.

GLITTER PIE
ART STUDIO

1789 Queen St E, Toronto, 647.435.6235
glitterpie.ca

Creative. Inspiring. Love.
Glitter Pie Art Studio bakes in The Beaches of Toronto and sprinkles glitter on the sidewalks
with love. An inspiring art studio space, Glitter Pie serves clients creativity in pretty,
recyclable packages. They work on custom commission pieces, create special curriculum for
those in need, and rescue most anything in an effort to beautify the world and keep things
green. Our mission is to show how to merge the "everyday" item or happening and give it
a little love and glitter and watch the world change one person or art project at a time.

Sandra Cowan

 Q and A

What are your most popular
products or services?
New digital lenses, Madmenesque
frames, RX polarized sunglasses.

People may be surprised to know...
Opticians are trained, licensed health care
professionals. Sales associates are not.

Who is your role model or mentor?
Auntie Mame.

What business mistake have you
made that you will not repeat?
Hiring a friend.

Where is your favourite place to
go with your girlfriends?
The Trane Studio for jazz.

GOLDSTEIN BOUTIQUE

171 1/2 King St E, Toronto, 416.368.9910
goldsteinboutique.com

Quirky. Stylish. Individual.
Goldstein Boutique opened in 1998 to offer a unique personal eyewear experience. There are no walls of frames or harsh lighting, just the benefit of Sandra Cowan's 25 years of experience and international scouting of boutique brands and up-and-comers. This is a one-woman show— no juniors. Sandra just shares her creative eye for which of 1000 frames is perfect for you.

Good for Her
175 Harbord St

Carlyle Jansen

 Q and A

What are your most popular
products or services?
Rechargeable designer vibrators, fun and
sophisticated sexuality workshops, adult DVDs
that appeal to women, luxurious oils, and
bachelorette/girls'-night-out home parties.

People may be surprised to know...
Parents are welcome! We have a kids'
toys and books area. We also have many
resources on parenting, kids, and sex.

What or who inspired you to
start your business?
My sister's friends. I gave sex toys to
my sister at her bachelorette party. After
answering numerous questions, they said
"You are so comfortable talking about
sex, you should teach workshops!"

GOOD FOR HER

175 Harbord St, Toronto, 416.588.0900
goodforher.com, Twitter: @goodforher

Fun. Stylish. Comfortable.
Good For Her is a sexuality boutique and workshop centre for women and their
admirers. They offer eco-conscious and quality sex toys, female-friendly adult
DVDs, and sexuality books in a warm, professional environment. Enjoy a cup
of tea and personalized service from the knowledgeable staff, attend renowned
sexuality workshops, or shop and learn online from the comfort of your home.

Photos by Jennifer Klementti Photography

Photos by IrinaPhotography

GRACE
ANNOUNCEMENTS

Toronto, 905.235.3032
graceannouncements.com, Twitter: @graceannounce, facebook.com/graceannouncements

Stylish. Modern. Unique.
Grace Announcements offers a complete line of professional photo birth and adoption
announcements, invitations, holiday cards, note cards, "call me" cards, personalized
wall art prints and placemats, and so much more. Grace Announcements takes great
pride in offering unique designs, photo editing, and unbeatable customer service.

Lindsay Brewda

What are your most popular products or services?
Our custom-designed photo birth announcements.
Customers love that they can have a card
that is trendy and unique, just like them.

People may be surprised to know...
When I was young, I dreamed of being
an interior and fashion designer.

What or who inspired you to start your business?
My son. When he was born, I realised there
was no way for me to announce him to the
world that also expressed me and my style.

What do you CRAVE? In business? In life?
An organised, clutter-free life. I don't know
if this will ever be attained while running
a business and raising two kids!

**What business mistake have you
made that you will not repeat?**
Not believing in myself. I held back on many things
I wanted to do because I didn't feel I was ready.

Nicolette Beasley

Q and A

What are your most popular products or services?
The Ultimate Italian Feast, the Gluten-Free Party, all of the chocolate gift baskets, and our gift customization service.

What or who inspired you to start your business?
While caring for relatives dealing with severe illness and then finding myself challenged with health and food allergy issues, I realised the need for gift baskets with delicious health- and diet-appropriate foods and treats.

What business mistake have you made that you will not repeat?
I hesitated to ask for help and advice, but I have come to find that people are more than willing to share their expertise.

HEALTHY GOURMET GIFTS

Toronto, 416.918.1072
healthygourmetgifts.com, Twitter: @hgourmetgifts

Decadent. Wholesome. Modern.
Healthy Gourmet Gifts takes a fresh approach to gourmet gift baskets, offering premium quality foods and treats selected for decadent, guilt-free indulgence. Unique selections include organics, kosher, allergen-free, and low GI items, supporting wellness for those with special dietary needs. Healthy Gourmet Gifts are elegantly presented in modern, re-usable, and eco-friendly totes, bags, boxes, baskets, and trays.

Celina Ainsworth

People may be surprised to know...
We lovingly hand-make many of our natural herbal medicine and skin-care products on site.

What or who inspired you to
start your business?
I did some of my herbal medicine training at Napier's Dispensary in Edinburgh. This was a fantastic experience that definitely inspired me.

How do you spend your free time?
During winter, I love to cook and keep cosy by the fire with my family. Summer months are spent outdoors in my gardens.

What do you CRAVE? In business? In life?
Doing what I love everyday and believing in what I do is what I crave. I enjoy what I do, and I admire all the people associated with my business—it's all good.

THE HERBAL CLINIC AND DISPENSARY

409 Roncesvalles Ave, Toronto, 416.537.5303
theherbalclinicanddispensary.com

Green. Natural. Unique.
A visit to The Herbal Clinic and Dispensary is a unique experience for anyone interested in herbal medicine and complementary healthcare. This beautiful "apothecary style" dispensary also provides high-quality practitioner services, including homeopathy, naturopathy, Bowen therapy, re-connective healing, registered massage therapy, psychotherapy, and community acupuncture in the adjacent clinic rooms. Fully qualified herbalists are available to assist in the dispensary.

Who is your role
model or mentor?

"*Margaret Thatcher,
who said:
'Being powerful
is like being a
lady. If you have
to tell people you
are, you aren't.'*"

Marina Bogdanova of Sweetings

HEYDOYOU

Toronto, 818.288.6746
heydoyou.com, Twitter: @heydoyou

Cute. Clever. Connected.
HeyDoYou is a lifestyle blog based in LA and Toronto. It is a marketing portal that amplifies word of mouth marketing. The site offers a marketer, a stylist, a writer, and a chef, plus product reviews on fragrances, beauty trends, gadgets, restaurants, movies, shoes, music, and events.

Bella Mumba, Yvonne Kai and Shay Ironmonger

Q and A

What are your most popular products or services?
Event coverage, sponsored posts, banner advertising, and product reviews.

What or who inspired you to start your business?
We started trending 10 years ago and just kept on blogging! Bloggers have an influential voice in the world where we are constantly surrounded by numerous adverts, events, and products. HeyDoYou finds the crème de la crème so you can just savour and be inspired.

How do you spend your free time?
I never have vacations because I live the life I want every single day. It is not about suffering and then rewarding, it's way more streamlined for me in my life. It's a constant flow of neon bursts of inspiration.

Who is your role model or mentor?
Carrie Bradshaw!

Cassidy Watkins

Q and A

What are your most popular products or services?
Fresh, local, organic toppings and, um, ... pizza! We also offer spelt and gluten-free options that are very popular with people with diet sensitivities.

People may be surprised to know...
Baking one of our pizzas is simple. You don't need any special tools. We provide everything that's needed. Also, organic multi-grain pizza dough can taste really good!

What business mistake have you made that you will not repeat?
I'm not really one to toot my own horn, which is a challenge, because having a new business necessitates you being able to let people know how fantastic it is.

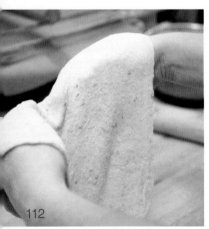

THE HOMEBAKE PIZZA COMPANY

476 Roncesvalles Ave, Toronto, 416.588.4272
homebakepizza.ca, Twitter: @homebakepizza

Fresh. Delicious. Gourmet.
The HomeBake Pizza Company is Toronto's first "take and bake" pizza shop.
Gourmet pizzas are made to order from all-natural, organic ingredients for
customers to take home and bake. HomeBake Pizza turns any home kitchen
into a gourmet pizzeria with the aromas of dinner, made easy!

HOT MAMAS FOODS INC

Toronto, 416.603.2468
hotmamas.ca, Twitter: @cdnpepperheads

Spicy. Unique. Vibrant.
Hot Mamas Foods Inc is a family owned, 100 percent Canadian business that makes
gourmet spicy pepper jellies, low sodium bbq sauces, marinades, no-salt spice rubs and
no-salt hot sauces, using only Scotch Bonnet peppers from Jamaica, as well as the family
farm in Pefferlaw. Hot Mamas offers a unique flavour and is proud of its Caribbean roots!

Sue Plumbohm

What are your most popular products or services?
Our customers and we agree that our Hot Mamas Spicy Red Pepper Jelly is the best on the market! Our hot sauces contain no salt and are healthy, tasty, and unique in the marketplace ... and very popular also!

People may be surprised to know...
Our products contain no gluten, preservatives, animal products, or artificial colours or flavours. We only use Scotch Bonnet peppers—and you'll taste the difference. There's nothing like it!

Where is your favourite place to go with your girlfriends?
Kicking back and relaxing at our family farm. A little wine—a little cheese—a little pepper jelly—bonfire—it's all good!

What do you CRAVE? In business? In life?
Success and happiness—that's what we all strive and work so hard for.

JANE HALL
THE VOICE OF STYLE

2156 Queen St E, Toronto, 416.691.8080
janehalldesign.com, Twitter: @janehalldesign

Unique. Vibrant. Personal.
The store has a full range of custom-made products designed by Jane and made by her elves. Almost everything is made from fabrics featuring European designers. Find custom-made lampshades, cushions, drapes, and "Janified" vintage and antique furniture. Jane Hall offers a full range of interior-design services, including colour consultations and renovation advice.

Photos by IrinaPhotography

110

Jane Hall

Q and A

What are your most popular products or services?
Repurposed vintage furniture, custom-made drapery cushions and lampshades, interior-design services, and colour consultations.

Who is your role model or mentor?
In 1976 when I first began at my kitchen table, there were no role models for me. I was a bit of a maverick, and I have been an entrepreneur for 34 years. I have been a role model for others starting out.

How do you spend your free time?
Being curious. Exploring all the things that fascinate me. Politics, sociology, culture, neuroscience, photography, social media, and new technology. I have now added writing to my "to do" list.

What is your indulgence?
Sleeping!

JUDY BLACK !

Toronto, Jen: 647.962.9225, Val: 416.435.0556
judyblack.ca

Original. Fresh. Contemporary.
JUDY BLACK ! is a funky and bright hand-printed apparel and accessories company.
They feature original hand-drawn images silkscreened on all-natural, organic fabrics using
water-based inks. Voila! One-of-a-kind pieces, limited edition and micro-collections are
all made with love and exceptional quality. All ingredients are 100 percent Canadian.

Jennifer Neill and Valerie Neill

Q and A

What are your most popular products or services?
Our most popular products are the half
hijab sweattop, acid sunset T-shirt,
and our famous circle purse.

What business mistake have you
made that you will not repeat?
Viewing mistakes as negative.

What or who inspired you to start your business?
Jen: Miles of printed fabric and sketchbooks full
of work. Val: Having the desire to be my own boss
and recognizing the potential of Jen's talent.

Who is your role model or mentor?
Jen: I've always tried to steer clear of
too much influence to keep my ideas
fresh and new. Val: My mom!

What do you CRAVE? In business? In life?
Success, freedom, health, spirit, and
something to call our own!

JUICY DESSERTS

Toronto, 416.602.9255
juicydesserts.com, Twitter: @juicydesserts, facebook.com/juicydesserts

Delicious. Memorable. Creative.
Juicy Desserts is dedicated to creating stylized cakes and cupcakes that are customized to match the theme of any special event. Each item is hand-crafted and designed to exceed your expectations by creating memorable and delicious desserts that will leave a lasting impression on you and your guests.

Josie Bancheri

What are your most popular products or services?
Wedding cakes and special event cakes.

People may be surprised to know...
I love quotes, and have several books
that I write them down in.

What or who inspired you to start your business?
My friend, Daniela, who believed in me enough
to ask me to make her seven tier wedding cake
even before I had ever made a wedding cake.

What is your indulgence?
Reese's peanut butter cups!

What do you CRAVE? In business? In life?
Fine details, laughter, creativity, ice
cream, photographs, simple pleasures,
love, knowledge, and chocolate.

How do you spend your free time?
I love to travel and get inspiration from
beautiful places I've never been.

Q and A

Katherine B. Toponiski

What are your most popular products or services?
Wedding photojournalism packages for 10 hours or more, uniquely personal family portrait sessions, and designer coffee table books.

Who is your role model or mentor?
My father taught me the foundations of photography; Henri-Cartier Bresson and Chien-Chi Chang inspire me creatively and in photographic approach.

How do you spend your free time?
I like being outside, walking, hiking, biking, exploring the city streets or nature with my camera; being social and silly.

What do you CRAVE? In business? In life?
I crave my camera! When I don't have it with me, I see photographs everywhere!

KBT PHOTOGRAPHY

Toronto, 416.704.1503
kbtphotography.ca, Twitter: @kbtphotography, facebook.com/kbtphotography

Genuine. Vibrant. Creative.
Katherine Toponiski combines her passion for photojournalism and artistic nature to create unique documentary-style photography. With an intuitive, natural approach, she focuses on building trust, comfort, and a connection with clients. Dedicated to photojournalism, Katherine photographs weddings; engagements; maternity, family, and lifestyle portraits; musicians, artists, businesses and professionals; and documentary projects. Through KBT PHOTOGRAPHY, she is available for bookings/assignments in Toronto and internationally.

KIDS AT HOME INC.

2086 Queen St E, Toronto, 416.698.9726
kidsathome.com

Unique. Inspiring. Vibrant.
Kids At Home is dedicated to making a child's space as unique, inspiring, and unforgettable as they are. Whether you are a tiny kid, little kid, or big kid, you are sure to find something you cannot live without. Each product in the boutique is carefully selected to ensure excitement in every kid and every parent.

Marg Gillespie

 Q and A

What are your most popular products or services?
Fatboy bean bag chairs, stunning diaper bags, custom linens, furniture for all ages, and an extensive array of wall art.

People may be surprised to know...
Kids At Home has interior designers on staff whose mission is to turn a child's space into everything they desire.

Where is your favourite place to go with your girlfriends?
There is nothing better than a cold glass of wine on the dock at the cottage while catching up on everyone's life.

What do you CRAVE? In business? In life?
The thrill of achieving the perfect fit, no matter how big or small the situation.

Elsie Hung and Joanie Yip

 Q and A

People may be surprised to know...
We used to carry fun dresses and did so
well that we opened a clothing store down
the street called Social Butterfly Boutique.

What or who inspired you to
start your business?
Our parents. Their entrepreneurial
background has definitely influenced
us to be our own bosses!

What is your indulgence?
Chocolates, shoes, and jackets.

What business mistake have you
made that you will not repeat?
Ordering too much of one thing.

How do you spend your free time?
Eating with friends and family.

LA DI DA BOUTIQUE

128 Danforth Ave, Toronto, 416.849.5388
ladidaonthedanforth.com, facebook.com/ladidaboutique

Fun. Stylish. Luxurious.
La Di Da makes gift giving effortless for that special someone. Whether it's
for a baby shower, wedding, birthday, or just-because, La Di Da has a wide
range of unique gifts. Be dazzled by the extensive jewellery collection.

LADY MOSQUITO

1020 Queen St W, Toronto, 647.637.9335
ladymosquito.ca, Twitter: @ladymosquito, facebook.com/ladymosquito

Flirtatious. Vibrant. Handmade.
Lady Mosquito launched in August 2008 with the mission of bringing to Toronto unique handbags, purses, and accessories from South America—truly beautiful and distinctive work. Since then, Lady Mosquito has formed partnerships with a range of young and super-talented designers, whose pieces add a bright kaleidoscope of South American colour to the already fascinating life and texture of Toronto's Queen West district.

Photos by conception design solutions

Cynthia Villegas

Q and A

What are your most popular products or services?
One-of-a-kind handbags and purses. Eco-friendly
accessories. Beautiful and unusual jewellery.

People may be surprised to know...
Every product we sell is handmade by
South American designers who own their
businesses and keep all their profits.

What or who inspired you to start your business?
Peru has an endless pool of wonderfully
talented designers. They inspired
me to start my own business.

What is your indulgence?
Fresh pineapple and lemon juice in the mornings.

What do you CRAVE? In business? In life?
When I can bring a real benefit to others by doing
what I love best—that's what makes me happy.

Clair Sutton

Q and A

What or who inspired you to
start your business?
Cooking has always been one of my greatest
loves, but my inspiration for baking came
later on with the guiding touch and gentle
hand of my dear friend Lena, who opened
my heart to the world of baking. Without
her none of this would be possible. Becky
Caulford and Michelle Quance, two of the most
influential ladies in my life. They are the most
beautiful, courageous, and talented ladies I
know, and their inspiration and strength has
guided me in the last three years. Without
the loving support of Mitsou, John, and Dave,
my dreams would have never come true.

What are your most popular
products or services?
We are known for our Earl Grey tea
with Mandarin icing cupcakes. Every
day we have an assortment of up to
12 flavors of all-natural cupcakes.

LIFE IS SWEET

2328 Queen St E, Toronto, 416.698.0555
lifeissweet.ca

Scrumptious. Delightful. All-natural.
Life is Sweet is a cupcake house tucked away at the blissfully peaceful, cosy end of Queen
Street East. The shop uses only natural ingredients for all of their products, including
cupcakes, brownies, scones, cookies, muffins, and lemon squares. Inspired by independent
women everywhere, owner Clair Sutton sees Life is Sweet as the perfect fit to combine
her love of food with the neighborhood that has nourished her for most of her life.

LIFECYCLES WELLNESS

94 Cumberland St, Ste 805, Toronto, 647.428.7200
lifecycleswellness.com

Vital. Nurturing. Inspiring.
At Lifecycles Wellness, the specialty is women's health care, such as menstrual, pregnancy, and fertility challenges. Owner Tanya Smith's passion is to empower women to live their healthiest lives through gentle, proven, holistic care using traditional Chinese medicine. As a woman, she understands the complexity and sensitivity of these health issues. Using lifestyle counselling, painless acupuncture, and herbal medicine, she creates the opportunity for healing.

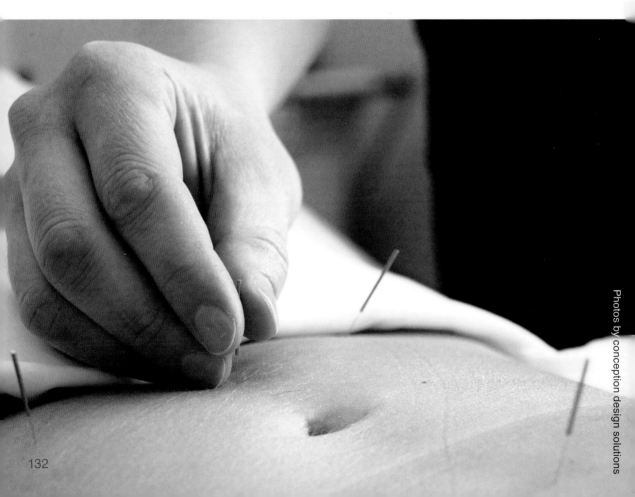

132

Photos by conception design solutions

Tanya Smith

 Q and A

What are your most popular products or services?
Acupuncture and Chinese herbal medicine for women struggling with painful periods, PMS, or fertility challenges. I also see many pregnant women for induction of labor.

What business mistake have you made that you will not repeat?
Early on, I didn't always take clients through the true value of the lifestyle suggestions I make as part of their care. I offered the information without the "why," and clients didn't always follow through and receive the benefit of that part of the treatment.

What is your indulgence?
Dance class. Shiatsu therapy with Guiomar Campbell. Chocolate from SOMA. Coffee from Crema. A day at body blitz.

What do you CRAVE? In business? In life?

"No matter what stage of life I am in, I want to see the world through a lens of gratitude and humility."

Gillian Johnson of Maae Jewelry and Accessories

Karyn Gingras

 Q and A

People may be surprised to know...
I really wanted to be a professional tap dancer.

Who is your role model or mentor?
I am inspired by the design and
independence of Elso Schiaparelli.
She had fierce personal style.

What business mistake have you
made that you will not repeat?
Not delegating. No one is an island. You
have to let go of control sometimes and trust
your staff to communicate your vision.

How do you spend your free time?
I travel to as many places as I can
with my sweet road bike, seeing
the world on two wheels.

What is your indulgence?
Vintage jackets, architecture
books, and anything Bakelite.

LILLIPUT HATS

462 College St, Toronto, 416.536.5933
lilliputhats.com

Classic. Modern. Artisanal.
Lilliput Hats is Toronto's only full-service traditional millinery. Celebrating two decades in business, Lilliput Hats continues to be the go-to place for fine hats, headpieces, bridal, special occasion, and casual funky styles. Each hat is handmade on site from the finest materials. The expert staff can help you find the perfect hat!

Photos by KBT PHOTOGRAPHY

137

LILOO AT HOME

734 Queen St E, Toronto, 416.466.8710
liloo.ca, Twitter: @lilooathome, facebook.com/lilooathome

Passionate. Vibrant. Inspiring.
Liloo at home is an Indian-inspired home décor and textile boutique offering beautiful bedding, luxury home furnishings, and unique personal accents. In addition to the home store, they also offer individualized gift-giving services, corporate gift services, wedding favors, event and home staging, linen rentals, and a private line of body care products and loose leaf tea.

Sapna Alim

What are your most popular products or services?
The most tempting item in our shop is
our bedding. In regards to the services
we offer, our corporate gifts.

People may be surprised to know...
That I play a mean air guitar.

What or who inspired you to start your business?
My deeply rooted desire for a connection
to India and my love of Indian textiles.

Who is your role model or mentor?
That's easy, my mom. She is more than
a mentor, she is my best friend!

What do you CRAVE? In business? In life?
What I crave the most in business is time.
There never seems to be enough. In life, it's
simple: love, happiness, and lots of chocolate.

What is your indulgence?
Pedicures and french fries.

Lily Setiawati

What are your most popular products or services?
Brazilians, cut, colour and highlights, facials with Eminence Organics and manis/pedis using SpaRitual vegan nail lacquers.

What or who inspired you to start your business?
My uncle in Java, Indonesia, who ran a huge, crazy salon and managed to please all the high-society women with great cuts and styles while also remaining a savvy entrepreneur right to the end.

What is your indulgence?
Extra-hot chili peppers. Large, unending quantities of them.

What do you CRAVE? In business? In life?
In business, to earn a great reputation and to keep attracting fun, interesting clients. In life, more free time for my beloveds.

LILY OF THE VALLEY

496 College St, Toronto, 416.913.3854
lilyofthevalley.ca

Friendly. Thorough. Professional.
In this cosy boutique hair salon/spa the attitude-free atmosphere sets the stage for near-painless and thorough Brazilians. The haircuts and styles make clients feel sexy and dangerous, and are engineered to last for months. Organic facials, soothing massages, and manis/pedis with vegan lacquer are gorgeous and stay perfect for weeks. Oh, and prices are quite reasonable.

Gillian Johnson

What are your most popular products or services?
Our textured silver and asymmetrical necklaces, bracelets, and earrings are the favourites with my customers.

People may be surprised to know...
That even though I make girly, sparkly jewelry, I am a tomboy at heart.

Who is your role model or mentor?
I have been lucky enough to be inspired by a number of different women in my life at different phases, and they have all imparted knowledge and guidance that has been useful along the way. And, of course, my mother, whom I named my business after!

What do you CRAVE? In business? In life?
No matter what stage of life I am in, I want to see the world through a lens of gratitude and humility.

MAAE JEWELRY AND ACCESSORIES

96 Spadina Ave, Ste 306, Toronto, 416.662.7824
maaejewelry.com

Funky. Feminine. Functional.
Maae Jewelry features a wide variety of designs made with natural stones, silver, gold, wood, and other exceptional materials handpicked from markets in Thailand and other international locations. With the distinctive combination of these materials, their handmade jewelry is characterized by original designs and vibrant colour combinations that allow women of all ages to express themselves in different ways, depending on the occasion!

Lorraine Hawley

 *Q and A*

What are your most popular products or services?
Triple chocolate brownies, peanut butter fudge cookies, and free-range chicken noodle soup.

People may be surprised to know...
You would never find buckets of mayo or pie filling at Mabel's. When we say "made from scratch," we mean it!

What or who inspired you to start your business?
Growing up on a farm, eating fresh and local, as well as living in France and seeing the passion for food.

Who is your role model or mentor?
My husband, a telecom entrepreneur and the hardest-working, most passionate man I know.

MABEL'S BAKERY & SPECIALTY FOODS

323 Roncesvalles Ave, Toronto, 416.534.2333
mabelsbakery.ca, Twitter: @mabelsbakery

Fresh. Delicious. All natural.
Mabel's is Roncesvalles' go-to specialty food shop for scratch-baked homestyle desserts and meals to go. Time-tested seasonal recipes are handmade with natural ingredients. Mabel's sources local and organic ingredients whenever possible and carries a selection of Ontario's best pantry items, artisan breads, and fine cheese.

Sarah Hamel

What or who inspired you to
start your business?
Toronto studio jewellers needed a space to
create, to interact with each other, and to sell!

Who is your role model or mentor?
These days, Michael Jackson—
he was all about *love*, creating
change, and being an artist.

How do you spend your free time?
Playing Lego with my 8-year-old son, Simon.

What is your indulgence?
Going to Body Blitz Spa ...
truly, a heaven on earth.

Where is your favourite place to
go with your girlfriends?
Any fromagerie with wine,
olives, and other nibbles.

MADE YOU LOOK JEWELLERY

1338 Queen St W, Toronto, 416.463.2136
1273 Queen St W, Toronto, 416.516.9595
madeyoulook.ca

Brilliant. Real. Fun.
Made You Look represents more than 100 Toronto jewellery designers. They are this city's hub for contemporary, innovative, unique, creative, one-of-a-kind, local, handcrafted jewellery. What's more, they have 20 independent designers creating jewellery right on site! Visit the stores, meet the artists, and have a piece of custom jewellery made especially for you!

MADELEINES, CHERRY PIE AND ICE CREAM

1087 Bathurst St, Toronto, 416.537.3131
madeleines.ca, Twitter: @madeleinescafe, facebook.com/madeleinescherrypieandicecream

Delicious. Memorable. Charming.
A feeling of comfort and desire to return defines the quality standard that makes Madeleines a sweet shop to remember. Pastries, bonbons, party planning, and custom-designed cakes round out this boutique patisserie's repertoire and their reputation for attention to detail. Whether you host your event in the cafe or engage Kyla's services to customize your occasion, your wedding, anniversary, birthday, or everyday event will be sweeter!

Kyla Eaglesham

Q and A

What are your most popular products or services?
Our most popular desserts are our
homemade pies and our signature five-
layer cakes. Parties are our specialty.

People may be surprised to know...
We have hosted three weddings and many special
events in our turn-of-the-century sweet shop.

What or who inspired you to start your business?
My energetic, creative, fun Mom. She has
operated a resort for 30 years and still
finds time to develop recipes with me.

How do you spend your free time?
I just started oil painting. I love the textures
you can create. It is a very inspiring meduim!

What business mistake have you
made that you will not repeat?
Not opening my own shop sooner. I worked in the
industry for 15 years before I opened Madeleines.

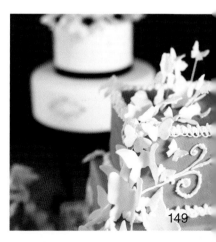

Shannon Doyle

Q and A

Who is your role model or mentor?
Jenny Barato, owner of Trattoria Giancarlo.
I admire her food knowledge and great taste.

What business mistake have you
made that you will not repeat?
Always secure a long lease or purchase
the building, if possible. It gives you
time to build your business.

How do you spend your free time?
Hot yoga and hosting dinner parties with my
husband when we are not renovating homes.

What is your indulgence?
Dark chocolate with sea salt and red wine.

Where is your favourite place to
go with your girlfriends?
Body Blitz Spa and Foxley Restaurant.

THE MERCANTILE

297 Roncesvalles Ave, Toronto, 416.531.7563
themercantile.ca

Gourmet. Unique. Urban.
A specialty food and treats shop, The Mercantile is chock-a-block with unique and delicious foods. When you enter the store, you feel inspired, indulged, and nurtured. The Mercantile is also a gift basket company beyond compare. Gift baskets are personally designed with each idiosyncratic recipient's needs in mind. The Mercantile: creating unique gift baskets for unique people since 1999.

MILLICENT VEE

55 Mill St, Case Goods Building #74, Studio #106, Toronto, 416.534.1399
millicentvee.com

Simple. Stylish. Comfortable.
Millicent Vee has been specializing in hand-knitted classic accessories, such as hats,
ponchos, wraps, and handwears for more than 10 years. Using luxury fibres, such
as alpacas, merinos, silks, and cottons, makes each piece unique and stylish.

Lori Dunn

 Q and A

What are your most popular products or services?
Hats and ponchos. I am always designing
new hats for the different seasons.
They are my favourite thing to knit!

People may be surprised to know...
Knits are not just for the winter. In the
summer, I keep a variety of lightweight
cotton/rayon accessories.

What or who inspired you to start your business?
Unhappily working for others. Knitting
since a child, I decided to go for it
and make it my profession.

Who is your role model or mentor?
Mary Quant, the designer behind the
mini-skirt. I re-read her autobiography
every few years for inspiration.

Laura Morris

Q and A

What are your most popular
products or services?
The Feng Shui Party, a custom in-home party.
It is a blast! It makes a great girls' night in.

What or who inspired you to
start your business?
I started my feng shui practice out
of a desire to be more mindful and
therapeutic in my work life.

How do you spend your free time?
Yoga—I try to find time to fit it in every day.

What is your indulgence?
Grande soy lattes.

What do you CRAVE? In business? In life?
Happy clients. I am grateful for being able
to help my clients find harmony, balance,
and positive energy in their lives.

MORRIS FENG SHUI

Toronto, 416.545.0015
morrisfengshui.com, Twitter: @morrisfengshui

Energy. Balance. Harmony.
Using a unique blend of classical and intuitive feng shui, Laura Morris works closely with her clients to revitalize their living spaces, increasing both energy flow and harmony. As a certified feng shui consultant and interior decorator, she uses her knowledge of space-planning, colour theory, and feng shui to assess a space. Her services include one-on-one feng shui consultations, group workshops, colour consultations, and space-planning.

Photos by conception design solutions

155

MS. LUBE BY MECHANCHIK INC.

499 Bathurst St, Toronto, 416.967.5823
mslube.com

Vivacious. Professional. Committed.
Ms. Lube by Mechanchik is the first and, so far, only all-female automotive repair facility in North America. Ms. Lube performs all services required by your car, and treats customers with the utmost respect and appreciation. The knowledgeable and friendly, all-female staff is here to serve you and your vehicle's best interests.

Jessica Gilbank

Q and A

What are your most popular products or services?
Our complete vehicle inspection that includes a proactive plan for you and your car is our most popular service.

People may be surprised to know...
We are the first all-female owned and operated auto repair facility in North America.

What or who inspired you to start your business?
Poor automotive repair experiences and the commitment to making the experience less overwhelming and frustrating for all consumers.

What is your indulgence?
Anything with a motor in it.

What do you CRAVE? In business? In life?
Making a difference in society's perception of the "old way" of things ... More female mechanics, doctors, lawyers, accountants, and CEOs. That's the goal. Change is good!

Gudrun Hardes

Charlene Sullivan

Q and A

People may be surprised to know...
We have been around for more than 10 years. Charlene opened Main St Cardio first, and Gudrun joined her five years ago. Business continues to grow.

What or who inspired you to start your business?
Both Charlene and Gudrun have taught fitness all their lives. It was just a natural progression to open our own studio.

How do you spend your free time?
Charlene is an avid nutritionist and loves to read everything about food. Gudrun loves to take yoga classes with friends. Of course our children are a big part of our lives and take up much free time.

What is your indulgence?
Gudrun loves travel, wine, and spa treatments. Charlene loves rock climbing.

Photos by conception design solutions. Charlene's portrait by Gudrun Hardes

MSC FITNESS
(MOVEMENT, SPIN, CONDITIONING)

2480 Gerrard Ave E, Toronto, 416.686.3545
mscfitness.com

Energy. Healthy. Innovative.
MSC Fitness offers more than 60 innovative classes each week including SPIN, hatha, vinyasa, power and yin yoga, Pilates, bootcamp, weights, kettlebells, TRX training, fusion (Piloga, Spoga), cardio groove, Bosu, step, ZUMBA, triathlon training, and nutrition. Great classes, great instructors, great energy, all in one great location.

People may be
surprised to know...

*Design and
decoration are
not frivolous,
nor are they arts
reserved for the
fortunate few.*

Erica Swanson of Erica Swanson Design

MY BUMP MATERNITY & MORE

944 Kingston Rd, Toronto, 416.698.6625
mybumpmaternity.com, Twitter: @mybump

Funky. Stylish. Young.
My Bump is Toronto's destination for great urban fashions for expectant and
new moms alike. With designers from Canada and around the globe, my Bump
offers expecting fashionistas and breast-feeding moms a wide range of urban-
chic clothing and accessories to dress up their bump or their new curves.
Be proud of your new curves and confident in your new skin!

Cheryl Atkinson

Q and A

What are your most popular products or services?
The Bella Band is one of the most popular
among first-time moms. A great pair of
premium maternity jeans is a must, followed
by a great nursing bra by Bravado.

People may be surprised to know...
Many breast-feeding styles accommodate
a growing belly! Breast-feeding clothing
is a great way to extend the life of
your wardrobe beyond maternity.

What business mistake have you
made that you will not repeat?
Taking my foot off the accelerator!
Business never stops.

What is your indulgence?
Boots—I have way too many.

What do you CRAVE? In business? In life?
I just want to be able to look back
and have no regrets!

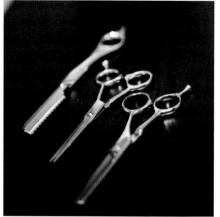

Nicole DeJong

 Q and A

What are your most popular
products or services?
I'd have to say the ICON
products; also Davines.

People may be surprised to know...
We are associated with Green Circle
Salons. They recycle all the hair
cuttings, foils, and colour tubes.

What or who inspired you to
start your business?
I wanted to create an atmosphere that would
inspire, soothe, and relax our clients.

What is your indulgence?
Chocolate. Can my trainer see this?

What do you CRAVE? In business? In life?
Always being passionate.

NICOLES HAIR STUDIO

2194 Queen St E, Toronto, 647.746.4247

Stylish. Talented. Zen.
Nicoles Hair Studio is a stylish, sleek salon in the heart of The Beach. Their team of stylists believe education is at the heart of the hair industry. Owner Nicole DeJong has created an inviting, relaxed environment and is dedicated to keeping her clients current and modern.

Karen Donaldson

Q and A

What are your most popular
products or services?
Our Ladies Only Indulgence Escapes, where
we bring the experience to you and our
signature ladies only event, "Urban Oasis."

What or who inspired you to
start your business?
I have had an entrepreneurial mind-set
from a young age when I began operating
as a freelance dance choreographer.

What business mistake have you
made that you will not repeat?
Putting marketing on the back burner.

What do you CRAVE? In business? In life?
To help people feel good about themselves—
the smile on their face is worth a million words!

How do you spend your free time?
When I do find some free time, I am all
about spending it with my family.

PANACHE LIFE INC.

Toronto, 416.414.2082
panachelife.ca, Twitter: @panachelife

Experience. Relax. Refresh.
Panache Life Inc. is a lifestyle and event-planning company dedicated to helping women live a lifestyle that nurtures and empowers. Panache Life Inc. takes care of every last detail for both simple and lavish events. They also boast a selection of indulgent escapes for you and your girlfriends: shopping parties with a personal stylist, nights on the town, alter ego photo sessions, and more!

Patricia Pinkney

 Q and A

What are your most popular
products or services?
Our harmony balls (earrings and pendants)
They are the jewellery piece that started
the business, and everyone loves them.

What do you CRAVE? In business? In life?
My personal aim is to do my part to enable
artisans, particularly women and those living
in emerging markets, to earn an income
through the practice of their craft. In my own
small way, I want my business to support
the livelihoods of these skilled artisans.
In many cases, their crafts are the living
expression of deep cultural traditions, and
I, along with the fair trade organisations
with which I work, believe in the importance
of the preservation of these cultures.

What is your indulgence?
Travel, of course, but also champagne,
a little habit I picked up in France!

PANGEA COLLECTION

Toronto, 416.498.1331
pangea-collection.com, Twitter: @pangeacollection, facebook/pangeacollection

Ethical. Cultural. Fashionable.
Pangea Collection features distinctive artisan, fair trade, and eco jewellery from around the world. The jewellery pieces are mainly from small, independent artisans, many of whom are women, living in developing countries. By purchasing their handicrafts, you are not only helping preserve deep cultural traditions, but also providing artisans with an opportunity to earn a living and achieve the art of self-reliance.

Photos by conception design solutions

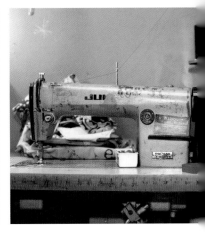

Kingi Carpenter

Q and A

What are your most popular products or services?
Colourful silk party dresses, patchwork hoodies, and silkscreen workshops.

What business mistake have you made that you will not repeat?
My biggest mistake in business was being a chicken! Never be afraid of rejection; it happens! Big deal! Move on!

What is your indulgence?
Cheezies, vodka, paint-by-number paintings, and MAC lip gloss.

Where is your favourite place to go with your girlfriends?
Our local restaurant, Java House, and anywhere in New York City.

PEACH BERSERK

507 Queen St W, Toronto, 416.504.1711
peachberserk.com, Twitter: @peachykingi

Flirty. Fun. Feminist.
Peach Berserk is funky, fun fabric and fashion design. They hand-print in their studio/store
with Kingi's original prints, and everything is sewn locally. Their colourful, witty clothes are
available off the rack or made to order. Pick the colour, style and print, and they make your
outfit to measurements. They love making custom prints, and offer silkscreen workshops, too!

Photos by Jennifer Klementti Photography

Photos by Calla Evans Photography

PERSONAL POWER IMAGE CONSULTING

Toronto, 905.988.9017
personalpowerimage.com, Twitter: @christieressel, facebook.com/personalpowerimageconsulting

Stylish. Fun. Chic.
Personal Power Image Consulting helps women feel more elegant, chic, stylish, and confident with personalized style coaching. Treat yourself by learning about style that works specifically for your personality, body type, lifestyle, and fashion! Personal Power Image Consulting also offers fun socializing services to do with your girlfriends, such as shopping with a stylist and makeup parties.

Christie Ressel

What are your most popular products or services?
Makeovers with a photo shoot, Fantasy Closet,
Colour Analysis, personal shopping, wardrobe
makeover, and blush, lashes, and lipstick.

What or who inspired you to start your business?
My own experience with image consulting
left me feeling so empowered! It's so much
fun and changed my life for the better.

How do you spend your free time?
Involving myself in something creative—I
love the arts! Daydreaming, reading, running,
shopping, and being with those I love.

What business mistake have you
made that you will not repeat?
In the beginning, I was afraid
to put myself out there.

Who is your role model or mentor?
My parents, Ogi and Linda, and my trainer,
Karen. Each are sources of light and inspiration.

Amy Saleh and Tanya List

$\mathcal{Q}$ and $\mathcal{A}$

What are your most popular
products or services?
Weddings and creative, beautiful
floral arrangements at all price points.
Even one flower can be stunning.

People may be surprised to know...
Being a florist is a workout.

How do you spend your free time?
Tanya likes to play soccer, basketball, watch
movies, and decorate her house. Amy likes
to golf, work out, and read everything!

Where is your favourite place to
go with your girlfriends?
A little neighbourbood bar called 2 Cats.

What do you CRAVE? In business? In life?
To balance work and life. Right
now, the business is winning.

PINK TWIG

PINK TWIG
FLORAL BOUTIQUE

711 College St, Toronto, 416.537.7465
pinktwig.ca

Beautiful. Fresh. Flirty.
Pink Twig Floral Boutique offers flower arrangements for all occasions, including a range of pricing, and delivery around the world. Wedding, corporate, and funereal arrangements, as well as gift baskets, are available. Pink Twig has been featured in *Wedluxe*, *Wedding Bells*, *House & Home*, and *Toronto Life*.

Barbara Snow DeAngelis

What are your most popular
products or services?
Exceptional quality loose leaf
tea and girlfriend gifts.

What or who inspired you to
start your business?
My mother.

People may be surprised to know...
We offer much more than just tea at Pippins.

How do you spend your free time?
With my dogs.

What is your indulgence?
Tea and chocolate!

Where is your favourite place to
go with your girlfriends?
Balsam Restaurant.

PIPPINS TEA COMPANY INC.

2098 Queen St E, Toronto, 416.694.7772
pippins.ca

Simply. Good. Taste.
Pippins Tea Company is an emporium of all things tea-related. Pippins offers tea lovers a diverse selection of more than 130 of the world's finest loose leaf and packaged teas, as well as delicious treats and a gallery of lovely teapots and accessories from around the world. It's the perfect shop for your everyday tea needs or an exceptional gift.

Q and A

What are your most popular products or services?
Lelo rechargeable vibrators, The Diva Cup, and Fertilitea (a tea for women trying to conceive).

What business mistake have you made that you will not repeat?
Trying to do too much! We quickly learned you can't be everything for everyone.

Where is your favourite place to go with your girlfriends?
Body blitz. There's nothing more relaxing than sitting in a pool of green tea and sipping a chai latte.

What or who inspired you to start your business?
Anita Diamant's novel, *The Red Tent*. We wanted to create a space where women could support one another.

Kim Sedgwick (co-owner Amy Sedgwick not pictured)

RED TENT SISTERS

810 Danforth Ave, Toronto, 416.463.8368
redtentsisters.com, ecosex.ca, Twitter: @redtentsisters

Healthy. Nurturing. Sustainable.
Red Tent Sisters is a cosy boutique run by two sisters who are passionate about women's sexual and reproductive health. The selection of eco-friendly sex toys, organic menstrual products, and holistic fertility support reflect a desire to offer women healthy, natural alternatives to mainstream products. Red Tent Sisters recently expanded to include an online store, ecosex.ca—Canada's first environmentally-friendly sexuality store.

Photos by KBT PHOTOGRAPHY

ROCKETFUELCOFFEE.COM

Toronto, 416.427.6674
rocketfuelcoffee.com, Twitter: @rcketfuelcoffee

Rare. Sensuous. Delicious.
Rocketfuelcoffee.com features rare, fresh-roasted coffee beans online: 100 percent pure Jamaican Blue Mountain, Hawaiian kona and their unique house blend, Rocketfuel Triple X. Rockefuelcoffee.com BLACK LABEL coffees include the rarest coffee in the world, genuine Kopi Luwak. Enjoy the finest coffees delivered right to your door by Canada Post.

Photos by KBT PHOTOGRAPHY

Lisa Rotenberg

 Q and A

People may be surprised to know...
These coffees are brought to Canada green and
roasted here in Toronto before shipping out to you.

What or who inspired you to start your business?
I am an illustrator who was looking for an
online business. I love coffee and each
coffee features one of my paintings on
the label. A cool pairing of interests!

What do you CRAVE? In business? In life?
In life, I crave really great shoes and boots.
And I will go around the globe to find them.

What are your most popular products or services?
Best sellers are 100 percent genuine
Jamaican Blue Mountain and Kopi Luwak.

What is your indulgence?
Single malt scotch and Cuban cigars.

RUELO PATISSERIE

550 Highway 7 E, Richmond Hill, 905.762.1500
ruelo.com

Trendy. Delicate. Sophisticated.
Ruelo Patisserie is a modern French pastry shop. They use premium, natural ingredients,
traditional French pastry-making techniques abd trendy dessert ideas to create a series
of six-star desserts. Ruelo Patisserie strives to make every piece a delicious surprise.

Jacqueline Lo

Q and A

What are your most popular products or services?
Macarons, the colourful almond meringue cookies sandwiched with anything from traditional caramel buttercream to outlandish flavoured ganache such as balsamic vinegar and wasabi grapefruit.

People may be surprised to know...
Ruelo is actually my name, in three ways: *rue* is "road" in French, and my last name, Lo, means "road" in Chinese. Ruelo is my road, or way, of pastry.

What business mistake have you made that you will not repeat?
I used to worry about the market, and I restricted my imagination when creating products. I found that when I have faith in my original creation, customers will come and buy.

What or who inspired you to start your business?
The beautiful pastry shops in Paris and Japan, and the heavenly treats within.

Cynthia Martyn

 Q and A

What are your most popular products or services?
Stephanie James Couture tea-length bridal gowns, Modern Romance silk wraps, and our birdcage veils.

What or who inspired you to start your business?
I have always known I would be an entrepreneur—I have been launching businesses since I was 12!

Who is your role model or mentor?
My mother has shown me the way with wisdom, grace, and style, and is a successful entrepreneur in her right.

How do you spend your free time?
I love exploring the city. I could drive around for hours discovering new boutiques and places of interest.

SASH & BUSTLE

233 Carlaw Ave, Unit 2, Toronto, 416.414.3617
sashandbustle.com, Twitter: @sashandbustle

Modern. Chic. Fresh.

Sash & Bustle is a fresh approach to bridal in Toronto. Located in an airy retail loft, the boutique is a haven for brides looking for beautiful alternative bridal gowns, chic bridesmaid dresses, and unique gifts and accessories. With a focus on a modern, simple aesthetic, Sash & Bustle is not your traditional "old school" bridal salon! The boutique also offers in-house wedding coordination services. Not only can you buy your dress and veil, but you can also hire a wedding day coordinator to ease your stress level on the big day.

Who is your role
model or mentor?

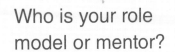*Mary Quant, the
designer behind
the mini-skirt.
I re-read her
autobiography
every few years
for inspiration.*

Lori Dunn of Millicent Vee

SENSE OF INDEPENDENCE BOUTIQUE

511 Eglinton Ave W, Toronto, 416.481.8242
senseofindependence.ca

Fun. Fresh. Sassy.
Sense of Independence is known for discovering new designers and featuring the latest trends before anyone else. Owners Naomi and Michelle couldn't wait to make their mark on the fashion world. With their combined fashion experience, they created a unique shopping experience that has drawn customers from around the city to get the latest and greatest in stylish clothing and over-the-top accessories.

Michelle Shamash and
Naomi Shamash-Veligman

Q and A

What are your most popular products or services?
Our tops and blouses selection. They are
easy to wear, can go effortlessly from day to
night, and have a fun twist to them, whether
printed, embellished, embroidered, etc.

What or who inspired you to start your business?
We've definitely inherited the shopping bug
from our mother and grandmother. We knew
from a young age that we wanted to work in the
fashion industry in one way or another. Coming
from a family of entrepreneurs, combining
business and fashion was a natural path for us.

How do you spend your free time?
We're always on the hunt for the next big thing.
You will probably find us reading through
gossip magazines or skimming gossip Web
sites to see what the celebrities are wearing.

SEW BE IT GIRL

282 Eglinton Ave W, Toronto, 647.347.6353
sewbeitgirl.com, Twitter: @sewbeitgirl, facebook/sewbeitgirl

SEW BE IT STUDIO

2156 Yonge St, Toronto, 416.481.7784
sewbeitstudio.com

Inspiring. Creative. Edgy.
Sew Be It Studio and Sew Be It Girl are committed to promoting the true art of sewing, fashion design, and fashion merchandising. Led by a team of experienced professionals, the studio offers an array of classes for all ages, genders, and levels of expertise.

Photos by IrinaPhotography

190

Lindsey Wise
and Dilys Tong

 Q and A

People may be surprised to know...
We create and work with young fashionistas to
bring their design visions into reality, whether
it's a dress for a bat mitzvah, sweet 16, father/
daughter dance, or any special occasion.

What or who inspired you to start your business?
Our friend, Courtney, who has a true flair for
fashion and an appreciation for simple, but unique
pieces. After months of teaching her to sew
her designs in Dilys' kitchen, over a glass (or a
few), we sparked the idea to start the studio.

Who is your role model or mentor?
Hilary Corbet, the previous CBC head of
design, who taught us all the sewing tricks.

What is your indulgence?
Shoes, shoes, and shoes! Nothing can complete
your wardrobe like a pair of sassy soles.

Denise Wild

What are your most popular products or services?
We offer sewing classes for all ages and skill levels, including beginner programs, refresher courses, fashion camps, and kids' classes.

What or who inspired you to start your business?
Sewing inspired me! It was my goal to do what I love and to teach it to others so that they would love it, too!

What is your indulgence?
Travel. I get restless without a getaway at least once a month.

What do you CRAVE? In business? In life?
I crave perfection, and I crave more! It's what keeps me going forward and makes me proud of what I do.

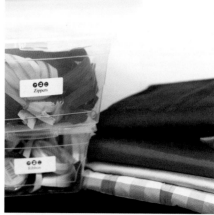

THE SEWING STUDIO

1225 Yonge St, Toronto, 416-901-0758
lovesewing.com, Twitter: @thesewingstudio, facebook.com/lovesewing

Creative. Fashionable. Fun.
The Sewing Studio is North America's leading sewing school. Since 2004, TSS has run sewing classes and fashion camps for newbies and stylistas alike. Their Web site is home to online sewing classes and video tutorials, as well as *LoveSewing*, a free monthly magazine that wears the title of the first sewing magazine to focus on fashion and style.

SHINY BITS

Toronto, 416.999.2303
shinybits.ca

Clean. Sophisticated. Modern.
Shiny Bits jewellery combines simple lines with dramatic appeal. Launched in 2008 by designer Amy Grisé, Shiny Bits offers wearable pieces that attract attention. The wide variety of sterling silver and silver plate designs make Shiny Bits both style- and budget-friendly. Their creations have made their way to countries worldwide, and to artisan shows across Southern Ontario.

Photos by conception design solutions

Amy Grise

 Q and A

People may be surprised to know...
I adore resale shops. I love finding a
deal on vintage and classic clothing
that I won't see on others.

Who is your role model or mentor?
My parents. They taught me a person can
go far with a good attitude, compassion,
confidence, and hard work.

What business mistake have you
made that you will not repeat?
Making jewellery that someone else
might like. I now embrace my own style
and make pieces that I truly love.

What is your indulgence?
I'm enticed by cheeses, desserts, and
anything salty. I dig in and choose
not to see it as an indulgence!

Photos by IrinaPhotography

SHOT IN THE DARK MYSTERIES

Toronto, 647.330.4678
shotinthedarkmysteries.com, Twitter: @mysterymaiden, facebook.com/shotinthedarkmysteries

Mysterious. Sassy. Unforgettable.
Shot In The Dark Mysteries' murder mystery and family-friendly mystery party games are the perfect solution for busy hosts, handing them the key to an unforgettable party their guests will rave about for years to come! Shot In The Dark Mysteries also offers Mysterious Marketing, which helps business owners connect with clients in a unique and unforgettable way.

Leigh Clements-Lynam

Q and A

What are your most popular products or services?
Custom games. We work our clients' inside jokes and intimate details right into the mystery plot!

People may be surprised to know...
I'm not as dark as some people expect someone who plots murder for a living to be.

Who is your role model or mentor?
Grace Kelly. She was class through and through and made her decisions for no one but herself.

What is your indulgence?
I have a great appreciation for a really good cup of coffee, and even the thought of shopping makes my heart beat faster!

What or who inspired you to start your business?
More than 40 jobs before the age of 25! Nothing taught me the importance of doing what I love better than being forced to do things I despised.

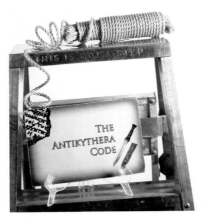

Melinda
Roopa

 *Q* and *A*

What are your most popular
products or services?
Soirée Toronto offers a complimentary
event-planning service. However, clients can
hire Soirée Toronto to either plan all or part
of their wedding, corporate, or non-profit
event or manage the day of the event.

People may be surprised to know...
All suppliers must pass a selection
process to be allowed on our exclusive
supplier list, ensuring they engage
in good business practice.

What is your indulgence?
Gummy bears ... my Kryptonite!

What do you CRAVE? In business? In life?
Positivity and *La Dolce Vita*.

SOIRÉE TORONTO

2573 Dundas St W, Toronto, 416.737.5164
soireetoronto.com, Twitter: @soireetoronto

Fresh. Positive. Inspirational.
Soirée Toronto is a complimentary event-planning service for anyone planning a
special event. They exist to educate the consumers through the entire planning
process. Soirée Toronto strives to *inspire* ideas, collaboration, and action by creating
memorable events, and *equip* clients with the plan to create *positive* experiences.
They are on top of the latest trends, events, and inspiration in the city.

Event Photos by Xero Digital Inc.

Jacqueline Parker

What are your most popular
products or services?
"Ooh la la!" is our new product section
located on our home page. We feature
products and services that our audience will
love. "Do It Solo" is also a great resource,
and our readers love the tips and advice.
The articles are impactful and not afraid to
address the issues single women face that
not everyone is comfortable discussing.

People may be surprised to know...
Our articles deal with lifestyle, and we
don't pretend to be relationship and dating
experts. We are more concerned about
other areas of women's lives that are just
as important and less spoken about.

Who is your role model or mentor?
I have several mentors. I've learned that
you can receive mentorship through so
many people around you who have had a
similar experience. It's very inspiring.

Photos by Jennifer Klementti Photography (face, bottom center and right (opposite page) by Heidi Geldhauser.

SOLOMAG

Toronto, 416.873.4958
solomag.com, Twitter: @solojacq, facebook.com/solomag

Insightful. Edgy. Refreshing.
Solomag is an online lifestyle magazine for single women offering great advice, resources, tips, and encouragement on a variety of issues that have impact on their daily lives, such as career, finance, real estate, relationships, travel, and learning to "Do it Solo."

Photos by Mari Blair, portrait photo by conception design solutions

STAGE FRIGHT

Toronto, 647.802.6274
stagefright.ca

Effective. Stylish. All-Encompasing.
Stage Fright is a full-service home staging and decorating company that stages/decorates "condos to castles" anywhere in the GTA and Durham. They offer stress-free property preparation for the real estate market, including: furniture, accessories, painting and lighting upgrades. Stage Fright can do everything from a basic consultation to top-to-bottom staging, and also offer decorating services, including colour consultations.

Mari Blair

Q and A

People may be surprised to know...
63 percent of people would pay more for a
"move-in ready" home, and homes sell 83
percent faster when they are furnished!

What or who inspired you to start your business?
My friend Michelle encouraged me to
look into home staging. She felt I had
the right skills, passion for decorating,
and service to be successful.

What business mistake have you
made that you will not repeat?
Undervaluing my hard work, and buying
furniture that doesn't fit through doorways!

How do you spend your free time?
I love going to the theatre, cooking, and having
dinner parties with friends, and especially hanging
out with my husband and our two daughters.

STEEPED AND INFUSED

1258 Queen St E, Toronto, 647.348.1669
steepedandinfused.com, Twitter: @steepedinfused

Healthy. Welcoming. Informative.
It's tea time! At Steeped and Infused, loose-leaf teas are the specialty. Their teas are carefully selected for quality, sensational taste, and, most importantly, their health benefits. Steeped and Infused offers a selection of premium creative blends that bestow warm and embracing aromas, a palate-pleasing finish and the refreshing awareness that you're doing something good for you!

Jennifer Best

Q and A

What are your most popular products or services?
Japanese Cherry, Herbs for Women,
Sweet Dreams, and cinnamon apple yogurt
blends, and our sample mixer gift pack.

People may be surprised to know...
Tea isn't just your grandmother's drink anymore.

What or who inspired you to start your business?
A journey with my health and the benefits
of tea provided the opportunity to combine
my two passions: health and business.

Who is your role model or mentor?
The community of amazing women
entrepreneurs that I am proud to be a part of.

What business mistake have you
made that you will not repeat?
Underestimating start-up costs; it costs more
than you think. Dismissing my intuition.

Fiona Liston

Q and A

What or who inspired you to start your business?
My grandfather was a head gardener at a country estate at home in Scotland and always encouraged me to be close to nature. He left a lasting impression on me, but truly, my partner, Matt, inspired me to live my dream.

Who is your role model or mentor?
Ercole Moroni from the prestigious McQueen's Flower School in London where I trained. His unconditional gift of knowledge was inspiring.

What do you CRAVE? In business? In life?
I crave the start of every fresh flower season, such as peonies in June, and the joy and excitement it brings to me and everyone in the store. I crave friends and family who are at home in Europe.

STEMZ

783 Queen St E, Toronto, 416.686.8526
stemz.ca

Stylish. Vibrant. Natural.
Stemz is a bustling flower shop located in the heart of Riverside. Bringing its own unique style and creativity to the neighbourhood, it seeks to bring a smile to the face of everyone who peers through its ever-changing window displays to see the creativity within. A focus on weddings and events keeps alive the creativity and unbound passion for flowers.

Photos by KBT PHOTOGRAPHY

Catherine
Chen

 Q and A

What are your most popular
products or services?
Ferrero Rocher cupcakes: pieces
of Ferrero Rocher mixed into a rich
chocolate cupcake, topped with Nutella
buttercream. True cupcake royalty!

What or who inspired you to
start your business?
An insatiable craving to share that
happy, nostalgic feeling you get when
biting into a fresh-baked cookie.

Who is your role model or mentor?
My mum, who taught me all the baking
basics, and to this day, still makes
the best desserts in the world.

How do you spend your free time?
Free time is rare, but I like to squeeze in a
workout or a little retail therapy when I can.

SUGAR BAKING

Toronto, 647.669.9754
sugar-baking.com, Twitter: @sugarbaking

Decadent. Sweet. Indulgent.
Sugar Baking creates custom, luxury desserts—delightful confectionery indulgences that taste as good as they look. Individual-sized treats add an extra flair to any occasion that will be appreciated by everyone, down to the very last bite. Sugar Baking offers delivery in the Greater Toronto Area, which makes it easy to satisfy that craving for something sweet.

Photos by conception design solutions

Sylvia Gamble

What are your most popular
products or services?
Buttercream cupcakes, Blossom
cakes, and the perfect hostess gift.

What or who inspired you to
start your business?
My independent spirit.

How do you spend your free time?
Walking by the water, cooking, and gardening.

Where is your favourite place to
go with your girlfriends?
Each others' homes for good
food, wine, and company.

What do you CRAVE? In business? In life?
Happiness and balance.

What is your indulgence?
A day off!

SUGARPLUM SWEET CREATIONS

1028 Kingston Rd, Toronto, 416.693.4747
sugarplum.ca

Sweet. Unique. Friendly.
This little gem in Kingston Road Village features freshly baked cupcakes and cakes hand-decorated with delicious buttercream frosting. Distinctly beautiful sweet creations are ready to go or custom designed. Plus, there is a special selection of unique gifts and greeting cards sure to match the importance of your special occasion. There is always a sweet find at Sugarplum: pretty treasures to give or to keep for yourself!

What is your indulgence?

"Pedicures, trashy chick-lit, really good cheese, and pie for breakfast."

Lorraine Hawley
of Mabel's Bakery & Specialty Foods

SWEETINGS

1920 Queen St E, Toronto, 416.686.6031
sweetings.ca

Elegant. Stylish. Friendly.
Sweetings offers sophisticated, elegant clothing from Italy and Europe.
Owner Marina Bogdanova shops with you in mind. She can help you build a
timeless wardrobe that will make you look and feel great everyday.

Marina Bogdanova

Q and A

What are your most popular products or services?
Clothing and accessories from Italy,
personal shopping, and styling.

How do you spend your free time?
On my couch, watching Fashion
Television, or with my children.

What is your indulgence?
Making my customers look and feel
great, and good coffee, of course.

What business mistake have you
made that you will not repeat?
Not opening sooner!

What or who inspired you to start your business?
The lack of well-made and unique, yet
affordable, clothing for women.

What do you CRAVE? In business? In life?
I would like to open more stores and
create my own line of clothing.

Kristen Gale

Q and A

What or who inspired you to start your business?
I've known I had to have my own business since I was 8. I love creating things, and this, paired with my passion for design, was the perfect fit for me.

What are your most popular products or services?
Our Brazilian is famed in the city. Following that, our pedicures and full facials at our unique facial bar are hugely popular. Plus we also offer "MANscaping" for the gents.

People may be surprised to know...
We toss away anything that isn't stainless steel and thus can't be sterilized. We special order our foot and nail files, which are sticker pads and only get used once!

What mistake have you made in your business that you will not repeat?
Listening to other people and not my intuition.

Photos by KBT PHOTOGRAPHY

THE TEN SPOT

749 Queen St W, Toronto, 416.915.1010
1402 Queen St E, Ste D1, Toronto, 416.915.1010
the10spot.com, Twitter: @thetenspot, facebook.com/thetenspot

Sassy. Sleek. Savvy.
The Ten Spot beauty bar is the city's ultimate "anti-spa" experience—manicures, pedicures, waxing, facials, and doin' gents is their specialty. Grab your gang or go solo and let them blow you away with their sleek style and savvy service. Screw "relaxation." This beauty and grooming boutique is all about a funky and fun experience. Plus, the Ten Spot is the hot spot for all kinds of private parties! Your guests can mix and mingle while being polished from top to all 10 toes.

THIEVES BOUTIQUE

1156 Queen St W, Toronto, 647.435.4880
thievesboutique.com, Twitter: @thievesboutique, facebook.com/thievesboutique

Edgy. Sustainable. Design.
Thieves Boutique is a men's and women's independent designer clothing boutique
that carries the house line, Thieves, as well as other fashion-forward, independent
designers that use sustainable materials and business practices. Thieves is locally
made, eco, edgy, and timeless, for the urban nomad on the move. The in-house
studio also provides the possibility of custom-tailored styles and sizes.

Photos by conception design solutions

Sonja den Elzen

 Q and A

People may be surprised to know...
We will often customize pieces from
the Thieves collections for clients.

What or who inspired you to start your business?
Growing up in an entrepreneurial
household, and the desire to actualize
my vision to share with others.

How do you spend your free time?
Practicing Zen Shiatsu, visiting friends,
dinners, exploring, travelling, going to art
shows, yoga, meditation, going to music
performances, dancing, and living.

Where is your favourite place to
go with your girlfriends?
Out dancing or to Addis Ababa Ethiopian
restaurant on Queen where we can sit
around, share food, and talk for hours.

THREE 16 LADIES BOUTIQUE

538 Eglinton Ave W, Toronto, 416.932.3823
three16.ca

Savvy. Stylish. Fun.
Three 16 is a chic ladies boutique in the heart of Forest Hill. Offering the perfect combination of fabulous clothing, stylish accessories, and friendly customer service, their stylists can help you mix and match pieces to create a well-functioning and fashion-forward wardrobe. Three 16 prides itself on the carefully selected trends it brings in from around the world.

Sabrina D'Amico

Q and A

What are your most popular products or services?
Our MICHAEL KORS line attracts a lot of attention.

What or who inspired you to start your business?
I've always had a passion for fashion,
but it was the female entrepreneurs
in my family who inspired me.

Who is your role model or mentor?
My husband. He's creative, hard-working
and extremely driven. That drives me.

**What business mistake have you
made that you will not repeat?**
I was so excited to open my doors that I didn't
take the time to properly consider my market.

What is your indulgence?
Milk and cookies in the middle of the night.

What do you CRAVE? In business? In life?
Success, longevity, and passion … for all things!

Savoy "Kapow!" Howe

Q and A

What are your most popular products or services?
Our recreational and amateur boxing programs. We also run a "Shape Your Life" program for female and Trans survivors of violence.

People may be surprised to know...
You never have to get hit in recreational boxing.

Who is your role model or mentor?
My coach, Toronto Newsboy "Razor" Ray Marsh, who has been my coach for 18 years.

How do you spend your free time?
Writing and working in theatre.

What do you CRAVE? In business? In life?
Grapefruit Moon's burger-in-a-wrap. To participate in the first Olympics for Women's Boxing in 2012.

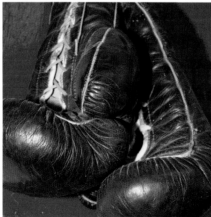

TORONTO NEWSGIRLS BOXING CLUB

388 Carlaw Ave, Ste 108, Toronto, 416.480.2058
torontonewsgirls.com

Positive. Safe. Empowering.
The Toronto Newsgirls Boxing Club is Canada's first all-female and Trans-positive boxing club offering recreational and amateur boxing programs for all levels of fitness. Their recreational program is ideal for those who have no desire to get punched in the nose! Their amateur program is very successful; recently they won three silver and three bronze medals at the 2010 Canadian Championships.

THE TRAVELLING TEACHER

Toronto, 416.871.7542
thetravellingteacher.com, facebook.com/travellingteacher

Passionate. Healthy. Inspiring.
The Travelling Teacher is an exhilarating and affordable dance and fitness company that has stepped out of the box, bringing a more creative and empowering approach to fitness and health. They offer classes in all styles, from Latin and ballroom, cardio, body sculpting, and boot-camp, to workshops, dancercise, private lessons, and hen nights! The Travelling Teacher travels to studios or anywhere in need of spicing up.

Jessica Willis

Q and A

What are your most popular products or services?
Latin classes and Argentine tango workshops. People love the sexy dances, so I keep adding more!

What business mistake have you made that you will not repeat?
Not starting my company sooner. If you know you can run it better than the people you are working for, do it.

How do you spend your free time?
Finding my country cottage online with chickens in the backyard, and taking my boyfriend out swing dancing!

What is your indulgence?
Food, food, and more food. One can never have enough good, expensive cheese and chutney!

People may be surprised to know...
I started in the singing/acting business and have a diploma in musical theater.

Shana Tilbrook, Louise Sommers
and Anita Owen

Q and A

People may be surprised to know...
Shana trains bra fitters across Canada
so they can provide the same level of
expertise in their own communities.

What or who inspired you to
start your business?
Having struggled from a young age to
find beautiful, well-fitting bras, Shana was
determined to help women in her situation.

How do you spend your free time?
Being a mum, Anita spends lots of
time with her kids. Louise loves to
study, and Shana dances salsa!

What do you CRAVE? In business? In life?
We want women to know that there's no
such thing as an "abnormal" size, and that
they can have beauty *and* comfort.

TRYST LINGERIE

465 Eglinton Ave W, Toronto, 416.484.6678
559 Queen St W, Toronto, 647.430.0994
trystlingerie.com, Twitter: @trystlingerie

Stylish. Knowledgeable. Friendly.
Tryst Lingerie, a family-owned business, carries bras and lingerie for all sizes of women. With two Toronto locations, they are known for expert fittings, quality merchandise, and superb customer service. A fitting at Tryst is a comfortable, no appointment necessary, experience. By carrying more than 150 bra sizes, Tryst has a variety of styles and shapes to complement all women.

Photos by KBT PHOTOGRAPHY

Myrlene Sundberg

What or who inspired you to
start your business?
I was an interior designer inspired by
European furniture but found very little
affordable modern design here.

Who is your role model or mentor?
My parents have always inspired me. I was
raised on a farm, and from that experience
I learned an amazing work ethic and
integrity that has shaped my entire life.

What is your indulgence?
Books, books, and more books. We have at
least 30 feet, floor to ceiling, of the best design
and architecture books from around the world.

What do you CRAVE? In business? In life?
I would love to be a part of a "sisterhood"
of women entrepreneurs. I have found it
to be very lonely. There is a lot that we
can share and learn from one another.

URBAN MODE

145 Tecumseth St, Toronto, 416.591.8834
urbanmode.com, Twitter: @urban_mode, facebook.com/urbanmodedesign

Modern. Multi-functional. Vibrant.
Urban Mode is Toronto's leading independent retailer of modern design and home furnishings and is regarded as the expert in small space management. Since 1977 Myrlene and her team have been showcasing new and noteable products from around the world. Passionate about design and architecture, Urban Mode has recently launched an eco-friendly, modular, pre-fab showroom adjacent to the store.

VINTAGE GARDENER

55 Mill St, Building 57, Toronto, 416.862.9500
vintagegardener.com, Twitter: @vintagegardener, facebook.com/vintagegardener

Tasteful. Fun. Current.
With a respectful nod to Grandma and celebrating a garden lifestyle, Vintage Gardener showcases an interesting selection of garden decoratives and well-chosen antiques. Throughout the gardening year, they host garden festivals and workshops in Toronto's gem, the historic Distillery District. At their studio, they create custom florals from the seasonal garden for your home, wedding, special occasion, gala, or corporate event.

Photos by IrinaPhotography

Elaine Martin

Q and A

What are your most popular products or services?
Our workshops are a great way to spend
a few hours with friends or friends yet-
to-be-met—always fun—and we have
never sent an ugly thing home!

What or who inspired you to start your business?
My daughter—definitely. This all started
as a hefty career change from the fashion
industry as a way to stay home with Anna.
Now she is in her 20s and a partner in the
business! You can see us on TV or YouTube
together—rather like "passing the spade."

How do you spend your free time?
A friend once suggested I find what I love
and do it—and well! I did! This makes it
difficult for me to know when work stops and
play starts. They are the same for me!

YORK PAINT AND DESIGN

Newmarket, 905.717.8123
facebook.com/yorkpaintanddesign

Fresh. Stylish. Fun.
York Paint and Design is a creative, personable painting company that puts pizzazz in your home. They will paint everything from basic wall colour to furniture. With their love of paint they will bring your personal style into your home. Check out some of their work on Facebook.

Lee Glavaz

What are your most popular products or services?
Our most popular services are children's
murals, basic wall colour application,
and colour consultations.

People may be surprised to know...
I actually have a background in
interior design and architecture.

Who is your role model or mentor?
My role model is Kim De Wolde of Cover
Your Windows. She has inspired me to
believe that no matter what business brings
my way, it can be conquered and we can
all succeed when working together.

Where is your favourite place to
go with your girlfriends?
I enjoy having my girlfriends over to my
home where we can sit back and enjoy
ourselves in a relaxed environment.

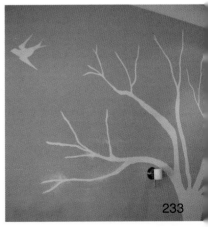

Zayna Mosam

Q and A

People may be surprised to know...
I work with people of all ages. Half of my clients are men, and I have special packages for couples and groups of friends.

What or who inspired you to start your business?
I wanted to make a difference in the lives of others on many levels. I also wanted the freedom to travel and to work with a variety of people in all industries, from the artistic to the scientific.

What business mistake have you made that you will not repeat?
Years ago, I carried out a large consulting project without a signed agreement. When the client refused to remunerate, I learned an expensive lesson!

ZAYNA MOSAM IMAGE CONSULTING

285 Manitoba Dr, Studio 5, Toronto, 416.907.8156
zmimage.com, Twitter: @zaynamosam

Strategic. Stylish. Instinctive.
Zayna Mosam Image Consulting was launched in 2003 and provides customized
programs for men and women, private groups, and corporations. Services include: image
and lifestyle management, communications coaching, etiquette and protocol coaching,
personal shopping, personal branding and styling, and public image development.
Zayna is a Certified Image Professional (CIP), speaker, writer, and frequent media
guest who has appeared on CTV, CityTV, MuchMusic, Bravo!, BNN, and more.

Intelligentsia Directory

Business-to-Business entreprenesses, including
coaching, marketing and public relations, photography,
business consulting, and design services.

THE CASSIDY PROJECTS

Toronto, 416.902.8092
thecassidyprojects.com, Twitter: @cassidyprojects

Creative. Dynamic. Innovative.
The Cassidy Projects is a strategic marketing and events company that specializes in cultural and socially innovative projects. Beginning with strictly events, The Cassidy Projects has evolved to offer its clients a variety of services from branding strategies to creative and business writing that answers the demands of the modern business mosaic.

Morna (MJ) Cassidy

Photo by Regina Garcia

Q and A

What are your most popular products or services?
Event strategizing, project management, and creative writing.

What or who inspired you to start your business?
I live in Toronto, a city that is largely defined by the freelance creative market that it supports. I wanted to be a part of that. I wanted to contribute to the coming-of-age of this great city through the unlimited opportunities of working for myself.

What business mistake have you made that you will not repeat?
Being confined by other people's ideas of what is possible. In the global market that we all operate in now, there really are no limits.

CHELSEA VIDEO VIBE

Toronto
chelseavideovibe.com, Twitter: @chelseavideo, facebook.com/chelseavideovibe

Edgy. Vibrant. Intuitive.
Chelsea Video Vibe (CVV) is a video production company that celebrates the best of urban life with energy, originality, and professionalism. CVV specializes in all things urban, from weddings and corporate functions to features on trendy, cultural happenings and sizzling charity events. Creating innovative, memorable accounts of life's special moments is their passion. Women and technology: inspiring and shaping the 21st century!

Photo by Peter Madison

Chelsea
Conway

Q and A

What are your most popular products or services?
CVV's most popular service is producing videos of trendy, cultural features, memorable charity events, and life's milestones.

People may be surprised to know...
I qualified to race at The Whistler Cup, an international ski competition, and sang solo at my high-school graduation.

What or who inspired you to start your business?
The female co-founders of The Society Global and courses and professors in my Ryerson radio and television degree program.

Who is your role model or mentor?
Family for support, wisdom, and confidence; Bruce Zinger and Colin Burwell for professional guidance; and Ivanka Trump for finesse.

DARE TO BE REAL
COACHING & CONSULTING

Toronto, 416.792.REAL (7325)
daretobereal.ca, Twitter: @menagagne

Authentic. Life-changing. Inspiring.
DARE TO BE REAL Coaching & Consulting specializes in increasing self-esteem in teen girls and women. Founder Mena Gagné is a passionate coach/speaker/workshop facilitator who "sees" individuals, invites the removal of "masks," expands perspectives, and creates a safe space for transformation. She empowers women to know, love, and be who they really are, encouraging them to emerge as authentic, confident, and courageous leaders.

Mena Gagné

What or who inspired you to start your business?
The catalyst for pursuing my purpose was a 10-month leadership program in California. I decided I wanted to have a positive impact on others' lives, and while it was scary, I was no longer willing to live with the pain of wearing masks in different areas of my life and feeling unfulfilled in the corporate world.

How do you spend your free time?
I love hanging out with horses—which is why I incorporate them into my work. They are calming, wise, and powerful teachers who show us what we might be blind to. I also love movies, yoga, dancing, manicures, pedicures, and reading.

What do you CRAVE? In business? In life?
Connections, love, contributions, learning, and fun!

ENTREPRENURSERY INC.

Toronto, 416.861.0990
entreprenursery.ca, Twitter: @entreprenursery, facebook.com/entreprenursery

Practical. Inspirational. Fun.
Launched and run by entrepreneurs and business women, EntrepreNursery Inc. is an entrepreneurial agency passionate about supporting the growing female entrepreneurial movement in Canada. Through workshops and ongoing consulting services, EntrepreNursery Inc., addresses the unique needs and challenges of women entrepreneurs from start-up to growth and beyond.

Liz Doyle Harmer

Gayle Campbell

Q and A

People may be surprised to know...
Gayle runs another successful business called Island Caribe, and Liz is a certified ashtanga yoga teacher.

What business mistake have you made that you will not repeat?
Spending too much time on service development and delivery and not enough time on marketing!

What is your indulgence?
Chocolate, wine, travel, and sleep.

Where is your favourite place to go with your girlfriends?
We both love trying new restaurants and enjoying the best of everything Toronto has to offer, from great sushi at Blowfish to veg fare at Fresh.

FATHOM COMMUNICATIONS

115 George St, Ste 1501, Oakville, 905.338.9348
fathomco.com, Twitter: @fathomco, facebook.com/fathomcommunications

Accessible. Streamlined. Forward-thinking.
Fathom Communications is a boutique public relations agency that helps brands rise to the surface. Working with a wide array of lifestyle clients in travel, home décor, culinary arts, health, and beauty, they have cultivated genuine relationships with the media, key influencers, and style makers who shape how the world views your brand among a sea of competitors.

Laura Johnston

People may be surprised to know...
I used to work on cruise ships before I went into PR. It provided the inspiration for our company name.

What or who inspired you to start your business?
My family. I come from an entrepreneurial background—it's in the blood!

Who is your role model or mentor?
Through example, my dad has taught me integrity, commitment, and the value of hard work.

What is your indulgence?
Travel, travel, and more travel! Once you've been bitten by the bug, it's hard to shake.

FOUNDATION STUDIO MARKETING & PROMOTIONS

11 Crittenden Dr, Keswick, 905.830.6243
foundationstudio.ca, Twitter: @fdnstudio, facebook.com/foundationstudio

Creative. Authentic. Dependable.

Foundation Studio specializes in high-impact marketing methods. They create social media personalities with pizazz, Web sites and blogs with zing, and brands that pop! Serving a diverse group of clients, from basement businesses to retail stores, Foundation Studio provides businesses affordable marketing solutions. Let Foundation Studio give your business a kick!

Photo by Studio 1948

Ariane Griffiths

What are your most popular products or services?
Web site, blog, and social media (Facebook and Twitter) design.

People may be surprised to know...
They can have an easily updated, great-looking Web site for less than $250.

What or who inspired you to start your business?
I saw the lack of affordable, quality services in my industry and wanted to fix it.

Who is your role model or mentor?
Women who really fight for their success; Anita Roddick, and Martha Stewart are some of my faves.

HEALTHYGIRL

Toronto
healthygirl.ca, Twitter: @leannegrechulk

Healthy. Happy. Holistic.
HealthyGirl is an online wellness destination for women entrepreneurs, guiding women in business toward optimal health through newsletters, events, e-books, grocery lists, and more. A panel of HealthyGirl experts is committed to keeping you in the loop with the latest health resources. Watch for an upcoming HealthyGirl Workshop in your city, and join the HealthyGirl community through their Web site.

Leanne Grechulk

 Q and A

What are your most popular products or services?
Holistic health coaching, nutritional products and programs, e-books, and our HealthyGirl seminars and events.

How do you spend your free time?
Travelling, running, yoga, swimming in the ocean, writing, reading, and creating ways to have more free time!

What business mistake have you made that you will not repeat?
Not setting clear expectations! In my experience, all mistakes and disappointments are a result of poor communication or unclear expectations. Be clear up front, and set your expectations from the beginning. I'm much better today! Secondly, it's so true that you must commit to excuses or results. Today, I'm 100 percent committed to results.

IRINAPHOTOGRAPHY

Toronto: 647.477.3995, Ottawa: 613.216.9601
irinaphotography.ca, Twitter: @irinafortey

Authentic. Vibrant. Artistic.
IrinaPhotography is a boutique photography studio in the heart of downtown, offering memorable experiences with each artistic and contemporary portrait session. IrinaPhotography's wedding clients appreciate the comprehensive approach in their creative and journalistic wedding collections. They believe that everyone deserves a set of beautifully designed prints, collages, storyboards, custom cards, and heirloom albums with each collection.

Photo by Kristina Laukkanen

Irina Fortey

Q and A

People may be surprised to know...
The sensitivity and care that goes into the creation of each photograph. We do more than simply document a story. We feel it too.

What or who inspired you to start your business?
My husband, Mihkel, has been the most inspirational person to my business. His love and support allowed me to grow.

How do you spend your free time?
I enjoy reading books, discussing history with friends, and enjoying the freedom and serenity of yoga.

What do you CRAVE? In business? In life?
There is a synergy between my photography and my life. My passion is my craft, and I want others to know that I put my heart into my work. I believe in honesty and integrity.

IT'S DUC

Toronto, 416.274.3708
itsduc.com, Twitter: @pgerochi

Elegant. Appealing. Engaging.
It's DUC is a Web development company founded by Peony Gerochi. The company
strives to create easy-to-use and clean Web sites, and prides itself on its diverse
client base, which recently expanded outside Toronto and across the border.

Peony Gerochi

 Q and A

What are your most popular
products or services?
Custom Wordpress themes, Web site
design, and front-end development.

People may be surprised to know...
I am in the works of starting another company.

What or who inspired you to
start your business?
My family and friends have played a big
part in my success. They have either
inspired, motivated, or encouraged me.

How do you spend your free time?
Learning more about the Web industry
to strengthen my skills and knowledge.
Otherwise, I play video games and
drums, and spend time with friends.

THE LITTLE BLACK DRESS AGENCY

2001 Erin Gate Blvd, Pickering, 647.241.5401
webstarts.com/thelittleblackdress, Twitter: @tlilblackdress, facebook.com/thelittlebackdressagency

Creative. Urban. Impressive.

The Little Black Dress Agency provides professional and experienced bartenders, wait/cocktail staff, models, and promoters to host your events, with the most stylish and enthusiastic ladies you will ever meet! The Little Black Dress Agency will go above and beyond to make a memorable experience for your guests so you can sit back and enjoy your event. Your guests will be more than impressed!

Kelly Flowers

 Q and A

People may be surprised to know...
I was a model for years, from fashion shows to billboards. I love the industry and would like to use what I have learned along the way to help other ladies become successful doing something they love!

Who is your role model or mentor?
Madonna. Anyone that knows me, knows she is my idol. She has created an empire, as well as a standard I'm not sure anyone else will ever meet. It is something I cherish and only hope to have one day for myself. Hard work and dedication will always pay off!

How do you spend your free time?
Any free time I have is spent with my 3-year-old daughter, Alyssa. A mini me ... she will take over the business one day!

LIZPR

Toronto, 416.544.1803
lizpr.com, Twitter: @lizpr

Professional. Chic. Fun.
LIZPR specializes in creating publicity and press kits for musicians, especially classical.
However, any business owner needs FABULOSITY in her promo materials, right? You need
a well-written bio or blurb, a few great headshots, a snappy mission statement, and catchy
Web copy. If you need an image re-vamp for yourself or your business, check out LIZPR!

Photo by Tara McMullen

Liz Parker

Q and A

What are your most popular
products or services?
Translating what you do into professional
promo materials—while conveying a strong
sense of who you are and what you do!

People may be surprised to know...
I'm a "Star Trek" geek. I joke about weird-
looking food resembling a "Klingon
buffet" or "Cardassian stew."

How do you spend your free time?
Perusing the shops—gotta know what's
current. Cooking. The Food Network is my
porn channel. I also read magazines a lot.

What or who inspired you to
start your business?
My dad always told me to "follow your
bliss." Nobody loved music more than
he did. He's always my inspiration.

MAHSAPPEAL COMMUNICATIONS

Toronto, 416.834.3866
mahsappeal.com, Twitter: @mahsappeal, facebook.com/mahsappeal

Attentive. Compelling. Vivid.
Mahsappeal Communications offers public relations, communications, and event coordination for your small business, non-profit, or start-up. The business was created with one goal in mind, to help small companies get the attention they deserve. They'll work with you one-on-one to determine your company's specific communication needs while staying within your budget, and they'll make a BIG deal of your small business!

Photo by Little Rock Designs

Mahsa Shamsipour

Q and A

What are your most popular products or services?
Our more popular services involve public relations, social media training, and editing services.

People may be surprised to know...
We offer photography as well.

What or who inspired you to start your business?
My passion for communications and helping small businesses inspired me. I always knew I wanted to run my own business.

How do you spend your free time?
At the gym, using social media, hanging out with family/friends, and travelling. I have a huge passion for travel.

MINDLESS SOPHISTICATION
WEDDING & EVENT PLANNING

1 First Canadian Pl - Toronto Board of Trade Tower, Ste 350, Toronto, 416.251.3278
mindlesssophistication.com, Twitter: @sophisticatewed, facebook.com/mindlesssophistication

Sophisticated. Unique. Vibrant.
Mindless Sophistication is a luxury wedding planning firm that offers full
planning, consulting, "day of" coordination, and customized prix-fixe destination
weddings. They also offer the Wedding Concierge®, an exclusive service
devoted to making sure out-of-town guests have an enjoyable visit.

What are your most popular
products or services?
Destination weddings and our wedding
day indulgence package, which provides
"day of" wedding or event coordination.

Who is your role model or mentor?
I am honoured to be a member of Sasha
Souza's Team I Do for the year 2010. Sasha
has been such a great role model as I expand
my business. She's always forthright with her
opinions. She's one of the top event planners
and designers in the world right now, so
being able to ask her questions and get no-
holds-barred answers has been amazing.

What business mistake have you
made that you will not repeat?
Not signing a contract with someone
I trusted. You have to have those
i's dotted and the t's crossed.

Sandra Aaron

MOTIVMODE

Toronto, 905.495.0582
motivmode.com, Twitter: @lydiafernandes

Authentic. Engaging. Fun.
MotivMode specializes in helping women unearth and leverage their authentic "wow factor" for professional and personal success. Using personal branding as a core strategy, they work with clients to build a competitive advantage while enabling a stronger sense of purpose and fulfillment. Company founder Lydia Fernandes is a certified personal branding strategist who values people and work/life synergy.

Lydia Fernandes

People may be surprised to know...
I am a founding case author for Hot Mommas®—the largest online library of female role models. I'm also married to an identical triplet!

What or who inspired you to start your business?
I needed to find a way to unleash my creativity and do meaningful, fulfilling work. Entrepreneurship opened that door for me.

Who is your role model or mentor?
My childhood ballet teacher had the perfect combination of poise, grace, and ongoing encouragement that boosted my confidence.

What business mistake have you made that you will not repeat?
Social media has been a great tool; however, making ample time for face-to-face interaction has been critical to my business.

PIGEON PAYABLE

Toronto, 416.628.3184
pigeonpayable.com, Twitter: @pigeonpayable

Reliable. Understanding. Respectful.
Pigeon Payable was created to facilitate collections of accounts receivable for sole proprietorships. Knowing that being the salesperson and accounting department is tricky and sometimes awkward, Pigeon Payable helps maintain relationships with your clients and follow-up on outstanding invoices for you. Like a carrier pigeon, they return your money to you.

 Q and A

Photo by Colektiv Images

Carlie Smith

People may be surprised to know...
Sometimes the hardest thing for people to do is pick up the phone, but it can make all the difference.

Who is your role model or mentor?
Richard Branson. He is the ultimate entrepreneur—and fabulous at empowering and managing his employees.

What business mistake have you made that you will not repeat?
Letting my costs get out of control. When things are good, it's easy not to analyze your costs and waste money that you miss when things get tough.

How do you spend your free time?
I dance modern jive with my fiancé!

PINK ELEPHANT
COMMUNICATIONS

Toronto
pinkelephantcommunications.com, Twitter: @prettypachyderm, facebook.com/pinkelephantcommunications

Thoughtful. Conscious. Lovely.
Pink Elephant Communications offers guilt-free marketing for the socially conscious. Their writers, designers, creative thinkers, and dreamers help entrepreneurs—artists and arts organisations, retailers, and holistic practitioners—promote themselves in a way that feels good, and allows them reach more people (and make more money). Woman-owned, they only print on eco-friendly papers, and their offices run on green energy.

Carrie Klassen

People may be surprised to know...
Marketing a business doesn't mean selling your soul. It can even be a force for good when done thoughtfully.

What business mistake have you made that you will not repeat?
I once hired a Web developer because he was charming. His work wasn't. Now I always check references.

Where is your favourite place to go with your girlfriends?
Coffee at Jet Fuel, cookies at Le Select, and the green tea pool at body blitz.

What do you CRAVE? In business? In life?
Beauty. I love the curling, wrought-iron fences of Paris and the elegance of a well-placed semi-colon.

Photo by Keith Klassen

POLY PLACEMENTS

Davisville Center - 1920 Yonge St, Ste 200, Toronto, 416.440.3362
polyplacements.com, Twitter: @polyplacements

Friendly. Transparent. Fresh.
Launched in 2006, Poly Placements is now No. 6 on the Profit Hot 50 list of companies—making them one of the fastest-growing recruitment companies in Canada. Why? Because their clients know that 97 percent of the hires they make through Poly Placements are still on the job—and succeeding—12 months later.

Photo by Pierre Gautreau Photography

Virginia Poly

Q and A

Who is your role model or mentor?
Richard Branson is a great example of how companies can change the world for the better—and have fun doing it.

What business mistake have you made that you will not repeat?
Assuming that there is only one way to build and grow a company. There are many different ways to be successful.

Where is your favourite place to go with your girlfriends?
An afternoon at Stillwater Spa, followed by lychee martinis.

What do you CRAVE? In business? In life?
I crave the same thing in business and life: to be just a little bit smarter today than I was yesterday.

PUNCH!MEDIA

Toronto, 647.272.5588
punchmedia.ca, Twitter: @punchmediadotca, facebook.com/punchmediadotca

Passionate. Positive. Polished.
Whether it's through traditional mass media or online social media campaigns, PUNCH!media generates credibility and exposure for businesses. With more than 10 years of experience in marketing and sales for Tier 1 clients, such as Visa Canada, PUNCH!media is deeply passionate about helping businesses succeed. By educating and empowering entrepreneurs through workshops and strategy, PUNCH!media helps create and build buzz for their brand.

Leslie
Hughes

 Q and A

What are your most popular products or services?
Social media seminars and strategies, press release creation, and media kit development.

People may be surprised to know...
I also run Diaper Disco, the hippest family dance party for the under-12 crowd and their ultra-cool parents.

What or who inspired you to start your business?
I was inspired to start PUNCH!media because of my passion and desire to see other businesses succeed.

What do you CRAVE? In business? In life?
Authenticity. I prefer to associate with businesses and people that are genuine.

SILVERBERRY OCCASIONS
EVENT PLANNING & DESIGN INC.

Toronto, 647.219.2871, 416.909.7329
silverberryoccasions.com, Twitter: @soeventplanning

Personal. Dedicated. Perfect.
Combine a true love and passion for all things event with fresh ideas and an artful eye for detail, and you get Silverberry Occasions Event Planning & Design Inc. Silverberry Occasions caters to clients of all types, from corporate to weddings and much more.

Photo by Purple Martini Wedding & Event Photography

Karen Chiavatti
and Jessica Wainberg

Q and A

What are your most popular products or services?
Our "day of" coordination. It's the perfect way to be hands-on with your event while still having the expertise of an event planner to guide you.

What or who inspired you to start your business?
Our previous experiences within the event industry left us wanting more. Starting Silverberry Occasions was the best way to combine our knowledge.

How do you spend your free time?
Checking out events in and around the city. It's a great way to meet new people and discover hidden gems.

What is your indulgence?
Wedding magazines! We're always looking for inspiration and fresh ideas, and we can't get enough of the real-life love stories.

255

SUGAR

Toronto, 416.260.1824
sugardesign.ca

Passionate. Driven. Focused.
Sugar is a multi-disciplinary graphic design studio that believes clients shouldn't have to chew cane to enjoy the flavours of tasteful design. Whether it's building brands or creating your online presence, Sugar provides clear, creative thinking for even the most complex challenges. Contact Sugar to find out how they can sweeten your communications.

Photo by Nikki Ormerod

Katina
Constantinou

Q and A

People may be surprised to know...
Sugar also offers brand consulting.
Beyond look and feel, the thought
of completely influencing the entire
direction of a brand really excites me.

What or who inspired you to
start your business?
I wanted a life where creativity wasn't
edited. I wanted to run with ideas
and push design boundaries.

Who is your role model or mentor?
I'm inspired by passionate people, period.
The ones that take charge of their creativity,
those who push the envelope, and allow
their work to become part of who they are.

How do you spend your free time?
Free time is hard to find these days, but when I
do have it, I'm training for the Iceland marathon.

TRIFECTA RISK MANAGEMENT SOLUTIONS, INC.

219 Dufferin St, Ste 220C, Toronto, 416.306.6480
trifectarms.com, Twitter: @trifectarms.com, facebook.com/trifectarms

Insurance. Risk Management. Claims Advocacy.
Trifecta RMS' mission is to deliver superior insurance products across Canada by innovative, technologically-advanced, and creative means, in an ecologically and socially responsible manner. Think "green". Trifecta is a trusted risk management advisor that works with clients and fellow brokers to develop competitive, tailored insurance programs, and provides risk management consulting designed to compliment each client's unique business needs.

Photo by Christine Miranda-Frias

Ateeya Lail

Q and A

What or who inspired you to
start your business?
A profound desire to truly innovate in an
industry requiring a fresh perspective
paired with a good friend's wise words.

Who is your role model or mentor?
My father, who taught me to live
without fear, love without condition,
and dream without limitations.

What is your indulgence?
All Apple products—anything with
the Apple logo, and I'm sold.

Where is your favourite place to
go with your girlfriends?
Mildred's Temple Kitchen in Liberty Village—
best gourmet burger in town, service
with a smile, and a little controversy.

UCREE8

Toronto, 416.220.2164
ucree8.com, Twitter: @ucree8

Smart. Trusted. Motivated.
UCree8 helps independent business owners manage their business needs.
Keeping the business side of a company in order can be quite a daunting task,
especially when all you want to do is focus on your job. UCree8 takes care
of the tedious business obligations, so you can focus on creating.

Vera Sethna

 Q and A

What are your most popular
products or services?
Bookkeeping, connecting clients to
services that fill their needs (grants,
manufacturers, competitors, Web designers
etc.), and advice/consultations.

Who is your role model or mentor?
Everyday people. Hearing their journey
and struggles of what they've had to
overcome drives me to strive for more.

How do you spend your free time?
Working! I love what I do. Socializing
and networking are also on the list.

Where is your favourite place to
go with your girlfriends?
Trying new restaurants, either
for brunch or dinner.

YOGAGURL

Toronto, 416.818.YOGA (9642)
yogagurl.com, Twitter: @yogagurldotcom

Playful. Health conscious. Visionary.
The Yogagurl mission is to foster a playful, balanced outlook on life. Owner Alexandra Leikermoser was the the first to create a mobile yoga team, bringing Y.A.M. (yoga, art, and music) to you! Discover fun tools to cope with stress and change. If you share the vision, Yogagurl would love to have you join their growing team of Yogagurl franchisees.

Alexandra
Leikermoser

 Q and A

People may be surprised to know...
I was nominated No. 1 in the top four yoga-wear designers in Canada, as well as one of the thousand most creative women in Toronto in 2009.

What or who inspired you to start your business?
Yogagurl was born out of my desire to attain personal clarity and balance after burnout as an eco-interior designer. "Yoga Girl" and "Guru" were my nicknames, thus "Yogagurl" was born!

What do you CRAVE? In business? In life?
I crave connections with genuine people and being in the moment. Generating wealth through playfulness. Loving life! Teaching people how to do this for themselves at my retreats.

YOUR FAB VA
A VIRTUAL ASSISTANCE COMPANY

Toronto, 647.500.3843
yourfabva.com, Twitter: @yourfabva, facebook.com/yourfabva

Innovative. Savvy. Fabulous.
Outsourcing is a proactive approach that can improve your company's productivity. Your Fab VA offers expertise to help you manage your business. Think of them as your online business manager. With a genuine interest in your business, Your Fab VA provides you with quality assistance on an "as-needed" basis—perfect for the business that doesn't need full-time assistance.

Jocelyn Reyes
Midghall

 Q and A

What are your most popular products or services?
Assisting start-up businesses, solopreneurs and not-for-profits with their marketing efforts—specifically social networking, research, office administration services, events, and meeting management.

People may be surprised to know...
There are more than 30,000 VAs all over the world!

What or who inspired you to start your business?
I have always been an administrative professional and aspired to be a business owner. I had read about VAs in Tim Feriss' *4 Hour Work Week*. At a course, the speaker suggested I look into exploring being a virtual assistant.

Contributors

At CRAVE Toronto, we believe in acknowledging, celebrating, and passionately supporting locally-owned businesses and entrepreneurs. We are extremely grateful to all contributors for this publication.

Amanda Buzard
graphic designer and project manager
amandabuzard.com

Amanda is a Seattle–based designer inspired by clean patterns and bold textiles. She chases many creative and active pursuits in her spare time. Passions include Northwest travel, photography, dining out, and creating community.

Alison Peacock
copy editor
peacockweddings.com

Alison Peacock is a writer, editor, and photographer with 18 years of journalism experience. When she's not copyediting books about savvy businesswomen, she focuses her camera on her favorite subject: weddings.

Lilla Kovacs
operations manager
lilla@thecravecompany.com

Lilla has been with CRAVE since 2005. As the operations manager, she ensures that everything runs like clockwork. She loves shoe shopping, traveling, art, and her MacBook.

Nicole Shema
project manager
nicoles@craveparty.com

Nicole graduated from the University of Oregon in June 2009 with bachelor's degrees in economics and political science, and then moved back to her hometown of Seattle. She has been with CRAVE since September 2009.

Melisa Miller
intern
melisa@craveparty.com

Melisa is a young Seattle professional with a love for the printed word, as well as the art of printmaking.

Alison Turner
graphic designer
alisonjturner.com

Alison is a graphic designer, seamstress, and outdoor enthusiast from Seattle. She is a supporter of the ongoing push for human rights, as well as the local food movement.

Contributors (continued)

Calla Evans Photography
photographer
callaevansphotography.com

With an extensive background in editorial and documentary photography, Calla Evans blends honest reportage and stylized portraiture for breathtaking results. Her unique, personalized approach to photography is refreshing and inspiring.

IrinaPhotography
photographer
irinaphotography.ca

Irina Fortey is a wedding and lifestyle photographer whose work is best described as emotional and creative. She has been published in wedding magazines and has received several awards for her portraiture. Irina is an active member of WPPI.

conception design solutions
photographer
conceptiondesign.ca

Richelle Chapman provides clients with graphic solutions that work. With a passion for art and a career in design, she discovered her love for photography through traveling the world and capturing snapshots that freeze moments and places in a single image.

KBT PHOTOGRAPHY
photographer
kbtphotography.ca

Dedicated to photojournalism, Katherine B. Topolniski photographs weddings, engagements, maternity, family and lifestyle portraits, musicians, artists, businesses, professionals, and documentary projects.

DSF Imaging
photographer
905.866.3764, dsfimaging.ca

Since 1998, DSF Imaging specializes in event, commercial, personal, and product photography. Owner Doug Gardiner has also worked in the digital imaging department of large firms, and has shot high-profile events in the GTA. A proud father, he is happiest outside with his two boys, camera in hand.

Jennifer Klementti
photographer
416.951.1715, jenniferklementti.com

Jennifer Klementti is a portrait, lifestyle, and documentary wedding photographer and visual storyteller whose work is honest, emotional, and contemplative. Jennifer's lifestyle work has been published internationally.

A Guide to our Index

ABODE - Home/interior design related goods and services.
ADORN - Jewellery-related goods and services.
CHILDREN'S - Baby, children, and mom-related goods and services.
CONNECT - Networking, media, technology, and event services.
DETAILS - Miscellaneous goods and services.
ENHANCE - Spa, salon, beauty, fitness studios, and personal trainers.
SIP SAVOUR - Food, drink, and caterers.
STYLE - Clothing, shoes, eyewear, handbags, stylists, etc.
PETS - Pet-related goods and services.

Manifest by category

$\mathcal{M}$anifest by category (continued)

Manifest by category (continued)

Manifest Intelligentsia Directory by category

$\mathcal{M}$anifest by neighbourhood

$\mathcal{M}$anifest by neighbourhood (continued)

$\mathcal{M}$anifest by neighbourhood (continued)

Craving Savings

Get the savings you crave with the following
participating entreprenesses—one time only!

10 percent off

- [ ] Ayala Raiter Jewelry Couture
- [ ] The Big Stretch Yoga Centre
- [ ] BlushPretty
- [ ] Chatelet and Chatelet Kids
- [ ] Cheeky Monkey Cosmetics
      (online with code CRAVE)
- [ ] Continuum Modern Vintage
- [ ] Dr | stephanie
- [ ] Ella Minnow Children's
      Bookstore
- [ ] Ella+elliot
- [ ] Embrujo Flamenco Tapas
      Restaurant & Café Madrid Bar
- [ ] Erica Swanson Design
      (online with code CRAVE)
- [ ] Fuss Hair Studio
- [ ] Glitter Pie Art Studio
- [ ] The Herbal Clinic
      and Dispensary
- [ ] Hot Mamas Foods Inc.
      (online with code CRAVE)
- [ ] IrinaPhotography (online
      with code CRAVE)
- [ ] Jane Hall
- [ ] Juicy Desserts (online
      with code CRAVE)
- [ ] Kids At Home Inc.
- [ ] Lady Mosquito
- [ ] Liloo at Home
- [ ] LIZPR (online with
      code CRAVE)
- [ ] Madeleines, Cherry
      Pie and Ice Cream

10 percent off (continued)

- [ ] Mahsappeal Communications
      (online with code CRAVE)
- [ ] The Mercantile
- [ ] Morris Feng Shui (online
      with code CRAVE)
- [ ] MSC Fitness
- [ ] Panache Life Inc. (online
      with code CRAVE)
- [ ] Pangea Collection (online
      with code CRAVE)
- [ ] Sash and Bustle
- [ ] Sense of Independence
      Boutique
- [ ] Sew Be It
- [ ] Sugar Baking (online
      with code CRAVE)
- [ ] Sweetings
- [ ] The Ten Spot
- [ ] Thieves Boutique
- [ ] Three 16 Ladies Boutique
- [ ] Vintage Gardener
- [ ] York Paint and Design

15 percent off

- [ ] 69 Vintage
- [ ] Beaches Bakeshop & Café
- [ ] Bergo Designs
- [ ] Big Dog Bakery
- [ ] Body blitz
- [ ] C1 art space
- [ ] Corktown Designs
- [ ] Distill
- [ ] DRYSDALE & CO.
- [ ] Eko Jewellery
- [ ] Feather Factory

Craving Savings

15 percent off (continued)

- [ ] Femm (online with code CRAVE)
- [ ] Foundation Studio (online with code CRAVE)
- [ ] Girl Friday
- [ ] Good For Her
- [ ] Grace Announcements (online with code CRAVE)
- [ ] The HomeBake Pizza Company
- [ ] It's DUC (online with code CRAVE)
- [ ] KBT PHOTOGRAPHY
- [ ] La Di Da Boutique
- [ ] Lilliput Hats
- [ ] Lily of the Valley
- [ ] Maae Jewelry and Accessories
- [ ] Millicent Vee
- [ ] My Bump Maternity & More
- [ ] Personal Power Image Consulting (online with code CRAVE)
- [ ] Pink Elephant Communications (online with code CRAVE)
- [ ] Pink Twig Floral Boutique
- [ ] Pippins Tea Company Inc.
- [ ] Shiny Bits (online with code CRAVE)
- [ ] Steeped and Infused
- [ ] Tryst Lingerie
- [ ] Your FAB VA (online with code CRAVE)
- [ ] Zayna Mosam Image Consulting

20 percent off

- [ ] Blo Blow Dry Bar
- [ ] Blossom Bath & Body
- [ ] Danceology
- [ ] EntrepreNursery Inc. (online with code CRAVE)
- [ ] Frock and frock-head
- [ ] Imelda
- [ ] Healthy Gourmet Gifts
- [ ] MotivMode (online with code CRAVE)
- [ ] Peach Berserk
- [ ] Punch!media (online with code CRAVE)
- [ ] Red Tent Sisters
- [ ] Shot In The Dark Mysteries (online with code CRAVE)
- [ ] Urban Mode
- [ ] YOGAGURL (online with code CRAVE)

25 percent off

- [ ] Coco&Jules Boutique Ltd.
- [ ] DivaGirl Inc. (online with code CRAVE)
- [ ] Lifecycles Wellness
- [ ] Stage Fright (online with code CRAVE)

30 percent off

- [ ] Mindless Sophistication

50 percent off

- [ ] Toronto Newsgirls Boxing Gym